The Mighty Wave

The 1798 Rebellion in Wexford

Dáire Keogh
& Nicholas Furlong
EDITORS

FOUR COURTS PRESS

Set in 10.5 on 12.5 point Stempel Garamond
by Verbatim Typesetting & Design for
FOUR COURTS PRESS
Kill Lane, Blackrock, Co. Dublin, Ireland
and in North America for
FOUR COURTS PRESS
c/o ISBS, 5804 N.E. Hassalo Street, Portland, OR 97213.

A catalogue record for this title
is available from the British Library.

ISBN 1-85182-253-4 cased
1-85182-254-2 pbk

425973

The cover design by Jarlath Hayes is based on
Edward Foran, OSA, *The Battle of Oulart Hill*
(27 May 1798); courtesy the Augustinian Fathers, New Ross;
photograph by P.J. Browne.

Printed in Ireland by
ßetaprint, Dublin

Contents

List of Contributors

Thomas Bartlett, MIRA is Professor of Modern Irish History at University College, Dublin.

Brian Cleary is a local historian and regular contributor to Wexford historical journals.

Louis M. Cullen, MIRA is Professor of Modern Irish History and Fellow of Trinity College, Dublin.

Nicholas Furlong, FRSAI is President of the Wexford Historical Society.

Daniel Gahan lectures in history at the University of Evansville, Indiana.

Thomas Graham is joint-editor of *History Ireland*.

Dáire Keogh lectures in the History Department, University College, Galway.

Anna Kinsella is a local historian and a regular contributor to Wexford historical journals.

Kevin Whelan is Burns Library Visiting Professor, Boston College, Massachusetts.

Preface

The forthcoming bicentenary of the rebellion of 1798 will undoubtedly stimulate debate about the nature of the dramatic events of that year and their subsequent interpretation. It is hoped that this volume will facilitate this discussion by placing Wexford within a national context and making recent historical research accessible to a wide audience.

Accordingly, this volume brings together a collection of papers delivered to the inaugural Comoradh '98 conference in Wexford together with a selection of the proceedings of the first Byrne-Perry Summer School, both of which were held in 1995.

The editors are indebted to many who have facilitated this publication. We would like to express our gratitude to the contributors; to Bernard Browne, Charles Kavanagh and the Board and the Historians-Librarians advisory committee of Comoradh '98; to the Revd Walter Forde and the Committee of the Byrne-Perry Summer School; to Paul and Rachael Keogh, Seán Mythen, Emer MacHale, Angela Malone, Mark Woods and Dr Muriel McCarthy and the staff of Archbishop Marsh's Library, Dublin. Thanks must also go to Matthew Stout for his splendid maps and to Nicholas Robinson for permission to reproduce illustrations from his collection. Finally, we would like to thank Michael Adams and Ronan Gallagher of Four Courts Press for their patience and encouragement.

The Wexford Pikeman by Oliver Sheppard

Reinterpreting the 1798 Rebellion in County Wexford

Kevin Whelan

The 1790s is arguably the pivotal decade in the evolution of modern Ireland. It witnessed the emergence of popular Republicanism and Loyalism, of separatism, of the Orange Order and Maynooth College, and culminated in the 1798 Rebellion and the Act of Union of 1800, which defined subsequent relations between Ireland and Britain. The decade also presents a dynamic interplay between Irish and international forces, when what happened on the island was inseparable from a wider global setting. The 1798 Rebellion linked Ireland in very specific ways with America, France and Australia in particular, making a permanent and indelible contribution to the evolution of the Irish diaspora.

Seventeen-ninety-eight also cast a long shadow. The resonant and romantic names of Theobald Wolfe Tone, Henry Joy McCracken, Beauchamp Bagenal Harvey, Thomas Russell, Robert Emmet, Lord Edward Fitzgerald, Father John Murphy and Miles Byrne, amongst many others, were to reverberate down the echo chambers of Irish history. While physically defeated, they achieved a remarkable symbolic victory, which has ensured their undying fame.

If the 1790s can be seen as the pivotal decade in the evolution of modern Ireland, then an honest and accurate understanding of it is not just of scholarly interest, but has important implications for current political and cultural thinking. It is precisely because of its enduring relevance that 1798 has never passed out of politics and into history. A window of opportunity was opened in Ireland by the impact of the American and French revolutions: that moment was brilliantly seized by the United Irishmen who imaginatively created a vision of a non-sectarian, democratic and inclusive politics, which could attract and sustain Irish people in all their inherited complexities. Rather than seeing religious, ethnic and political diversity as a disabling problem, the United Irishmen saw it as a glorious opportunity to construct a wider, more tolerant and generous vision of Irish identity. Rather than grimly clinging to a divisive past, the United Irishmen sought to create a shared future. By facing into the future rather than the past, they wished to heal the hurts of Irish history in a brotherhood of affection. In their first declaration of principle, they stated:

> We have thought much about our posterity, little about our ances-
> tors. Are we forever to walk like beasts of prey over the fields
> which these ancestors stained with blood?

The enduring legacy of the United Irishmen was their efforts to bring
Dissenter, Anglican and Catholic together in a shared political project.
That generous project was deliberately derailed by counter-revolutionar-
ies in the 1790s, largely through the injection of sectarianism to break the
United Irishmen's non-sectarian appeal. We are still living in Ireland with
the consequences of that defeat. The United Irish project of an inclusive,
democratic, non-sectarian Ireland remains uncompleted: understanding
the reason for its momentous defeat in the 1790s can help us to ensure
that history does not tragically repeat itself in the 1990s. That is the principal reason why we should not consign the United Irishmen and the
1790s to the dustbin of history. Those who fail to understand their history are doomed to repeat it and in many ways, the political problems
which face us as a people and as a state today are rooted in the 1790s.

The political architecture of these islands is built partly on the Act of
Union as a foundation while the 1790s demonstrate the difficulties in
creating a politics capable of representing the Irish people and their
inherited complexities, in solving the perplexing Rubik cube of nation,
church, state, empire and class. The 1790s forces us to confront these
thorny issues, rather than naively wishing for their reconciliation or
transcendence. And in purely historical terms, the 1790s also has enormous claims on our attention, because it is a hinge decade, summarising
the eighteenth century and anticipating much of the nineteenth.

I

In understanding the 1790s, we must begin by emphasising the triple
divide in eighteenth-century Ireland between Anglican, Dissenters and
Catholics – first, second and third class citizens respectively. The
achievement of the 1782 Constitution seemed to mark a giant step forward in creating a more cohesive sense of Irish nationality – but that
optimism soon subsided over the vexed issue of admitting Catholics to
the political nation. Many advanced parliamentary reformers were
unwilling to take this dramatic step and the reform movement split acri-
moniously on this issue in the mid 1780s. By decade's end, the great
optimism unleashed by 1782 had collapsed into a sterile, sectarian stalemate.

The French Revolution's significance in Ireland was that it broke this log jam: it was for this reason that Wolfe Tone called it 'the morning star of Liberty in Ireland'.[1] The French Catholics – supposedly priest-ridden and despotic – had suddenly demonstrated their political maturity, leapfrogging Britain's much heralded 'Glorious Revolution' of the previous century in the pursuit of political liberty. The Irish lesson was glaringly obvious – and expertly expressed by Tone in his *Argument on behalf of the Catholics of Ireland*. If French Catholics could display their maturity, then so too could Irish Catholics. This demolished the conservative Protestant argument against admitting them to the political nation. The new political space opened by the French Revolution could then be occupied by a non-sectarian political movement – the United Irishmen, bringing together the hitherto disparate agendas of parliamentary reform and Catholic Emancipation. The United Irish project was to create a reformed Irish parliament, free of its corrupting English connection: because it would be a representative parliament on American and French lines, it would command the full support of all Irish people, not just a sectarian-based faction. The reformed parliament would then be able to enact laws which would be the basis of a modernised Irish nation.

In their composition and ideology, the United Irishmen drew on a wide range of influences – English Whiggery, the Scottish Enlightenment, American Constitutionalism and the French *philosophes*. However, there was also a significant indigenous ingredient: the United Irishmen did not spring fully formed from the French Revolution, like Athena from the head of Zeus. It was precisely in the welding together of these traditions that the novelty of the United Irishmen lay. The diversity and reach of these formative influences is a caution against adopting a cabbage-patch approach to Ireland in the 1790s. What happened in Wexford or Antrim, Kildare or Armagh, cannot be separated from what was happening elsewhere in the Atlantic world at this stage. Ireland must constantly be inserted into this wider political picture if we are to have a proper perspective on the 1790s.

Nor can we forget the changing context, once France and Britain went to war in February 1793. This polarised opinion between those who supported and opposed the French Revolution, eventually squeezing out the middle ground. The British fear was that Ireland might become a strategic soft underbelly for the French. Therefore, Ireland must be kept on a tight leash. These concerns intensified in the aftermath of the Bantry Bay episode (December 1796) and the embarrassing mutiny at the Nore and Spithead in the following spring. Only if we understand the full ferocity of anti-French sentiment in British conservative opinion can we understand the equal ferocity with which the rebellion was treated in Ireland.

Edmund Burke had produced a nightmare vision of the French foul-
ing the whole nest of European civilisation:

> The revolution harpies of France, sprung from night and hell, or
> from that chaotic anarchy, which generated equivocally 'all mon-
> strous and prodigious things', cuckoo-like, adulterously lay their
> eggs, and brood over, and hatch them in the nest of every neigh-
> bouring state. These obscene harpies, who deck themselves in I
> know not what divine attributes, but who in reality are foul and
> ravenous birds of prey (both mothers and daughters), flutter over
> our heads, and souse down upon our tables, and leave nothing
> unrent, unrifled, unravaged or unpolluted with the slime of their
> filthy offal.[2]

And here were the United Irishmen coolly and deliberately inviting these
monsters into Ireland.

II

In Wexford, the French Revolution bisected pre-existing divisions within
its political culture.[3] There was no monolithic 'Protestant' or 'Catholic'
grouping in the 1780s. The Protestants, even in the absence of a
Dissenting interest, were split between conservatives (managed by Ely
and Ogle) and liberals (notably the Colclough-Grogan-Harvey interest).
County Wexford, with its eight borough and two county seats, was an
important political prize which was pugnaciously contested. Ely, a con-
summate borough monger and adept practitioner of patronage, controlled five of the borough seats – including one in Wexford town which
he and Neville carved up between them. This interference (followed by
wholesale creation of dubious freemen) was deeply resented by the liberals. Their unease intensified in the 1790 election when Ogle switched
from his independent stance to being pro-government. After that, both
Ely and Ogle were hate figures for the liberals and their Catholic allies –
especially as each became zealots in defence of 'Protestant Ascendancy'.
  When the United Irishmen were founded in Dublin in 1791, the
Wexford liberals joined them – notably Bagenal Harvey, William Hatton,
Samuel Cooper and Anthony Perry. This group was to stay the radical
course right through the 1790s – as well as being joined in the United
Irishmen by other leading Protestants like Matthew Keugh, Henry
Hughes, Nicholas Grey, John Boxwell and George Sparks. In the
Wexford context then, it is crucial to note that there was no homogenous

Protestant response to the events of the 1790s, and that its political class was deeply riven in its response to the French Revolution. Even so well-connected a figure as John Colclough of Tintern Abbey may eventually have sworn the United Irish oath.[4]

Moreover, it is crucial to note that the Catholic response was equally divided – a division which erupted in public over the Catholic Convention of 1792. Bishop James Caulfield, the senior clergy and other Catholic leaders sought to downplay Catholic dissent.[5] They were outflanked by younger activists like Edward Hay, James Edward Devereux and Edward Sweetman – all recently returned from France, all related and all keen to develop a confrontational politics. They also sought to isolate the recalcitrant clergy, as Caulfield bitterly complained:

> The spirit of [Wexford] town is now violent beyond belief and a general sullenness pervades. It seems to be the plan adopted to give the clergy nothing if they do not come into their measures.

Writing to his mentor Archbishop John Troy in Dublin, Caulfield proposed that the Catholic Committee be excommunicated for daring to pronounce on Catholic teaching, noting that 'it was a happy epoch indeed when the people, the puppies, the rabble dictate'.[6] But the radicals triumphed both nationally and in Wexford. John Keogh dismissed the bishops as 'old men used to bend to power, mistaking all attempts for liberty as in some way connected with the robbery and murders in France'.[7] He proceeded to threaten them with 'the French cure' if they refused to back the Catholic Convention – which Troy and the other bishops were forced to do. In Wexford, a younger, assertive generation took over Catholic leadership from their fathers – including Hay, Devereux, Edward Fitzgerald, Matthew Sutton, William Kearney, Thomas Cloney and Robert Meyler. From their activities in radical Catholic politics, they gravitated to the United Irishmen. Based in Wexford town, they made common cause with the pro-Catholic liberals against the diehard Ely-Ogle camp. Many of these Catholic leaders were educated on the Continent, were very familiar with France, and wished to achieve a similar freedom in the civil sphere for Irish Catholics. Mostly in their twenties, they represented a generation who had been raised after the American Revolution, and who welcomed the French Revolution as offering a fast-track solution to the problems of Irish Catholics.

But this was not just a radical clique of aspiring politicians. They achieved impressive feats of political mobilisation in the county as a whole. Sweetman could tell Wolfe Tone on 17 January 1794 that in

Edward Sweetman	Edward Sutton	Thomas Richards	Solomon Richards	Christopher Richards	Pat Prendergast	Robert Meyler	Matthew Keugh	William Kearney	John Johnstown	Edward Hay	William Harvey	Bagenal Harvey	William Hatton	Cornelius Grogan	Nicholas Grey	James Edward Devereux	Isaac Cornock	Samuel Cooper	Year	Name
		●	●	●			●	●						●	●		●		1776	Anti Whiteboy
		●		●	●		●	●							●				1779	Anti Importation
											●			●	●					Volunteer
	●	●		●	●		●						●						1781	Legislation
	●			●	●	●	●										●		1782	R.C. Charity
	●			●			●						●	●			●		1783	Grogan Vote
	●			●					●										1787	Wexford Petition
	●			●			●	●	●										1789	Robbery
							●						●	●					1790	Independent Elector
							●							●			●		1791	Wexford Town
●		●		●			●				●	●	●	●	●		●		1792	Freeholder
●			●											●			●		1792	Freeholder
		●	●				●				●	●	●	●			●	●	1792	Independent Freeholder
●	●			●				●									●		1792	Robbery
●	●					●		●		●					●				1792	R.C. Comm.
	●				●	●		●												T.O.S.F.
				●			●		●		●	●	●							Friends Const. Liberty and Peace
			●				●				●	●	●						1793	Grogan Vote
●											●	●						●		United Irishman
		●		●		●	●	●									●	●	1793	Reward Robbery
	●	●					●				●	●	●		●		●		1793	Anti Militia
			●				●			●			●		●		●		1793	Wexford Association
	●							●		●							●			Catholic Qualif. Rolls
	●		●	●	●		●				●	●	●		●		●		1794	Bridge Commission
		●	●	●	●	●	●	●			●	●	●		●				1794	Bridge Sub.
	●	●	●				●	●		●	●	●	●	●			●		1795	Fitzwilliam
			●	●	●		●												1796	Maltser
		●				●	●										●		1797	Wexford Petition
						●	●	●	●		●	●	●	●	●			●	1798	**Rebel**

The evolution of radicalism in Wexford politics in the late eighteenth century

County Wexford 'the lower orders [are] all alive and would do anything'.[8] This politicisation was reflected in a number of ways. In 1792, there were 20,000 signatures to the Wexford petition for a Catholic Relief Act and in that year there was enthusiastic participation in the Catholic Convention elections. In 1795, 22,251 signed a petition calling for the reinstatement of Fitzwilliam as Lord Lieutenant and in 1797 Wexford was one of the very few counties with a sharply contested election.[9] It was during it, for example, that Thomas Cloney refused to toast George Ogle at a dinner, illustrating the extent to which public political divides had opened within Wexford society.[10] Right through the 1790s, the political temperature was constantly rising in Wexford while simultaneously a cohort of radical and Catholic leaders were cutting their political teeth, as the decade threw up issue after divisive issue (fig. 1). Therefore, when the United Irishmen reorganised as a revolutionary movement, they found a receptive response in Wexford.

That reorganisation began in 1795, dictated by the need to create a military structure, capable of assisting the anticipated French invasion force.[11] The new military constitution spread more quickly in Ulster than in Leinster, where the moderates resisted it initially. By the autumn of 1796, the reorganisation was finally in place in Dublin. By this stage, a further refinement of radical thinking had led to acceptance of the concept of an indigenous insurrection, which would be undertaken with or without French aid. That concept necessitated the shift in the primary focus of the movement from Ulster to Dublin and the crescent of counties surrounding it. To deliver a successful coup, Dublin was the critical target – the capital, the link with Britain, the nerve centre of communications, the economic and administrative hub of the country. That policy required a build-up of the United Irish organisation in the city and its hinterland, as well as a complete grafting of the *military* onto the *civil* structures of the movement. This aim was achieved in the new constitution of August 1797 which made the organisation more streamlined and flexible, while clearly delineating an effective military hierarchy.[12] This ranged from the townland-based 'simple' societies of 12 men (a platoon) to the 120-strong parish-based company, to the 1200-strong barony-based regiment, to the county army (embracing all the baronial regiments), commanded by an adjutant-general chosen by the Provincial Directory and responsible for liaison with it.

As well as building the Dublin city organisation, the United Irishmen also turned to strengthening their hand in the crescent of counties which circled the capital from Meath through Kildare and Wicklow to Carlow and Wexford. In Wexford, there was the pre-existing group of early United Irish activists but these were affiliated to the 'moderate' rather

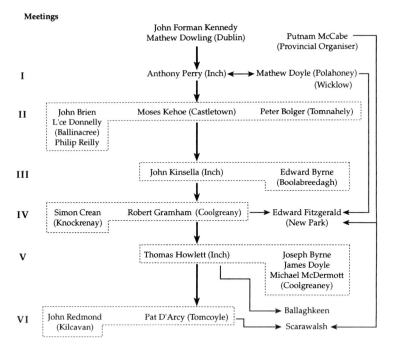

Figure 2: Organisation of United Irishmen North Wexford 1797–8

than the 'radical' wing of the movement.[13] The moderates did not wish to pursue a general insurrection in the absence of the French – while the radicals promoted the indigenous insurrection. The Wexford moderates, including Bagenal Harvey, Matthew Keugh, Edward Hay and Edward Fitzgerald, were slower in moving to the new fully military structure, with its system of small, interlocking, affiliated cells. Strong in the Wexford town and Forth and Bargy areas, these moderates acted as a significant brake on mobilisation there.

By contrast, the Dublin-based radicals began early in 1797 to proselytise North Wexford independent of the 'southern' Wexford leadership. Activists like William Putnam McCabe, James Hope and Charles Nowlan traversed the area from Castletown to Clonegal, establishing the new cell structure. Monaseed, for example, was organised in January 1797, Kilcormick in May and Clonegal in August. The new structure appealed to the rank-and-file and we can see its proliferation in the Castletown-Coolgreany area in 1797 (fig. 2). While Anthony Perry was a leading player, the key activists were artisans like Edward Byrne (a carpenter) and Michael McDermott (a blacksmith), as well as the pedlar Philip Reilly and the publican James Doyle. Paralleling and superimposed on this micro-

Hugh Keegan	Mason	Askakeigh
Patrick Keegan	Mason	Askakeigh
[—] Keegan	Mason	Askakeigh
Michael Connors	Blacksmith	Watch House
Whit Byrne	Maltster	Clonegal
Thomas Clarke	Slater	Ballyshonogue
William Clarke	Slater	Ballyshonogue
Jackie O'Neill	Farmer	Prospect
Dennis Beahon	Schoolmaster	Clonogan
John Mahon	Farmer	Drumderry
James Ryan	Publican	Clonegal
John Kenny	Labourer	Drumderry
John Short	Farmer	Carhill
Bryan Short	Tailor	Carhill
James Doyle	Carpenter	Ballyshonogue
Richard Quinton	Labourer	Garryhasten
Thomas Quinton	Labourer	Garryhasten
Thomas Connors	Carman	Ballyshonogue
John Keegan	Tailor	Clonegal
Daniel Doyle	Labourer	Clonegal

Figure 3: Clonegal United Irishman Activists, 1798

structure were wider links with Dublin (through Matthew Dowling and Putnam McCabe), with Wicklow (through Matthew Doyle), with the baronies of Ballaghkeen and Scarawalsh (through Thomas Howlett and Edward Fitzgerald). Strong farmers like the Darcys of Tomcoyle and the Grahams of Corcannon were also becoming active in the leadership structure of the baronial organisation. The popular appeal of the new organisation can be seen in the composition of the Clonegal cell of the United Irishmen (fig. 3), with its slaters, carmen, tailors, masons, blacksmiths and maltsters.

The rapid spread of the United Irishmen in North Wexford brought an anxious conservative response. While the liberals leaned towards the United Irishmen, the conservatives favoured tough measures but the county was effectively paralysed in security terms because no consensus was ever forthcoming. Into this stalemate came an opportunist politician – the Earl of Mountnorris, hoping to carve out a political space for himself within the polarised spectrum of Wexford politics. Having stood as a compromise candidate in the 1797 election, he also orchestrated an ostentatious display of Catholic loyalty in response to the proclamation of sixteen parishes in the north-east of the county on 20 November 1797. Using the chapels and priests as his organisational tools, Mountnorris was able to elicit an impressive series of loyalty testimonials from the

disturbed parishes. The map of those parishes which participated is effectively a map of the extent of United Irishman organisation in the county
by the winter of 1797 (fig. 4). The cells had now spread south along the
Macamore coast, and through the fertile mid-Wexford plains of Ferns,
Monageer, Oulart, Blackwater and Castlebridge.[14]

Despite Mountnorris' well-publicised efforts, the hard line loyalists
remained sceptical about the county's loyalty. By the spring of 1798 the
Dublin based 'cabinet' (Cooke, Fitzgibbon, Foster, Beresford) were all
convinced that only a policy of meeting rebellion (overt and covert) with
terror could 'lance the boil' of insurrection. They were especially anxious
about what they saw as the lax law-and-order policy in those counties
with a strong liberal or whig presence, especially Kildare, Wicklow,
Carlow and Wexford.[15] In an effort to create the nucleus of a hardline
law-and-order pro-government group in these counties, Dublin Castle
created new magistrates (who were all committed government supporters) and oversaw the transplantation of the Orange Order into the
region.

By May 1798, there were ten lodges in Carlow (associated with the
Rochfort and Cornwall interest), three in Wicklow (associated with
Stratford) and three in Wexford (associated with Hunter Gowan). Along
the Wicklow-Carlow-Wexford border, where the United Irishmen had a
strong footing, there were lodges at Clonegal, Tinahely, Carnew,
Coolkenno and Monaseed. Their spread generated great anxiety, as they
seemed linked to a much more repressive and sectarian security policy,
implemented by zealous and not over scrupulous magistrates like Robert
Cornwall (in Carlow), Hunter Gowan, Archibald Jacob and Hawtrey
White in Wexford. These illiberal magistrates were socially marginal or
outsiders, who quickly became the target of United Irish propaganda,
along with the new clerical magistrates like Revd Roger Owens, Revd
Standish Lowcay, Revd Thomas Handcock and Revd John Kennedy –
the visible embodiment of Protestant Ascendancy in church and state.

These men were also active in the yeomanry – controlling the most
sectarian, ill-disciplined corps in the county. As new men, and because
many of them (Gowan, Jacob, White) were middlemen, not landed
gentry, these figures were despised as upstarts by the richer, more established gentry in the county, like the Nunns, Richards and Carews, whose
profile remained liberal. That liberality was expressed in their yeomanry
corps, which were heavily Catholic in composition, even at the officer
level. For Dublin Castle and the hardline magistrates, these liberal corps
were seen as little better than United Irishmen by the Spring of 1798.
Their solution was to import the loyalty oath devised by General John
Knox in sectarianised mid-Ulster: each corps would be required to pub-

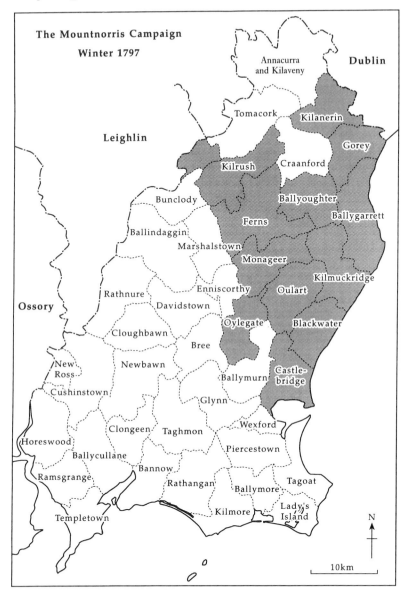

Figure 4: The Mountnorris Campaign, Winter 1797

licly and individually take the Oath of Allegiance and to declare their abhorrence of the United Irishmen. The suspect units (like Henry Grattan's 'Virgin Mary' corps in Wicklow, or those of his whig allies Hume, Edwards and Saunders) or Le Hunte, Richards, Cornock and Grogan in Wexford, could be especially targeted.

The liberal gentry opposed this 'test', seeing it as unconstitutional and invidious. The United Irishmen alleged that its real purpose was to prepare the way for yeomanry corps to join the Orange Order. In the volatile spring of 1798, it was a further turn of the screw in the increasingly tightly wound spiral of tension. A second wave of Mountnorris-inspired loyalty oaths by Catholic congregations accompanied this transition, inztensifying in late April as the situation on the ground deteriorated daily in north Wexford (fig. 5). This mirrored the national picture where the withdrawal of Abercromby allowed for the declaration of martial law on 30 March. This was followed by the first systematic government terror, in the Counties of Tipperary, Wicklow and Kildare. Mountnorris' ostentatious campaign may have kept Wexford out of this loop, but his attempt to stake out a middle ground was being crushed by the weight of polarisation.

Into this disturbed Wexford scene came a figure saddled with an immense baggage of myth and memory – Lord Kingsborough, the leader of the North Cork militia. His family had been centrally involved in the sectarian politics of Cork and Tipperary between 1758 and 1766, involving a witch hunt of propertied Catholics and culminating in the judicial murder of Father Nicholas Sheehy.[16] In later years, the family had become involved in a sensational scandal – the elopement of their daughter (allegedly corrupted by the feminist radicalism of her tutor, Mary Woolstonecraft) and the subsequent shooting dead of her lover by Kingsborough's father. The North Cork militia itself was an explicitly Protestant force – although well stocked with converts from the family's Mitchelstown estate. Kingsborough himself was a leading national figure in the Orange Order – like his friend George Ogle. It was presumably Ogle who arranged for the 600-strong North Cork militia to be stationed in County Wexford. When they marched there in late April, they publicly wore the Orange insignia, and thereby became a living, walking, embodiment of every Catholic nightmare. From their previous assignment in County Wicklow, stories had quickly spread of Kingsborough's preying on young females and the undisciplined behaviour of his men. They were soon to vindicate their ferocious reputation in Wexford by introducing the pitch-cap there.[17]

Ogle's eagerness to attract this unsavoury unit may have stemmed from the spring assizes of 1798 where the case against almost 100 United

Date	Location	Number of signatures
13 January	Clonegal	1,561
3 February	Marshalstown	500
13 February	Litter, Killincooly Monamolin	[1,000]
1 March	Kilrush	514
1 April	Ballycanew	773
18 April	Gorey	645
1 May	Castlebridge	150
	Kilmallock	170
	Kilmuckridge	834
	Ferns	1,500
	Kilanerin	1,360
	Kilcormick	757
	Ballynamonabeg	160
	Ballyoughter	800
	Ardamine	360
	Donoughmore	530
	Total	9,039

Figure 5: Numbers signing Catholic petition County Wexford 1798

Irishmen collapsed ignominiously in both Wicklow and Wexford to the delight of their colleagues. In the face of this legal impotence, the arrival of the North Cork militia was meant to stiffen the loyalist backbone and to give a signal that the leash would now be loosened on tough counter-insurgency measures. Gowan, Jacob and White were quick to grasp the implications and their yeoman units became increasingly aggressive throughout May.

But the arrival of the North Cork militia also strengthened the hand of the United Irishmen against the clerical opponents: they could now legitimately claim to be the sole defenders of the Catholics against real, visible and imminent threats. Priests could no longer pull back their congregations from wholesale involvement in the United Irish movement.[18] It is presumably at this stage, for example, that the wavering Father John Murphy pledged his allegiance to the United men. The arrival of the North Corks also coincided with the proclamation of the county on 27 April 1798, at yet another divided magistrates' meeting.

Over the border in Wicklow, where security had been placed by Dublin Castle in the hands of Joseph Hardy, an army man, the law and order policy was much tougher. Implemented by the Welsh regiment of Ancient Britons, it involved floggings, house burning and arrests. The few hardline magistrates were pleased at the result: 'the peasantry of the county are now the most humble creatures alive'.[19] In Wexford, though, there had been no significant arrests. The Government may have been distracted from the county by two events – the highly trumpeted Mountnorris campaign, and the fact that the Wexford United Irish delegate, Robert Graham, had arrived late for the famous meeting at Oliver Bond's house on 12 March. Avoiding arrest, he never gave in the Wexford membership figures, leading the Government (and many subsequent historians) to conclude that the county was not organised. Relatively unmolested, the United men continued to build their organisation right up to the eve of the insurrection, but with an increasingly urgent awareness that the day of reckoning was fast approaching. On 1 April 1798, Walter Devereux of Ballybrittas wrote to his brother in New York state:

> It is the greatest happiness to you that you left this unfortunate country, now the prey of the Orange and Castle bloodhounds. Almost every county in poor old Ireland under martial law and the poor country peasants shot or hanged or basteeled without law or any form of trial; all our respectable and honest country men in the gaols of our kingdom, such as Arthur O'Connor, Oliver Bond, Edward Fitzgerald, Sweetman the brewer and several others, but thank God, that Irish men have resolution and can suffer more and will be free. I would send you a more full account only that I hope it will not be long until it will be known and praised throughout the whole world. Dear John, send no remittance to Ireland until you learn of her freedom, and then, when you do, your honest friends shall only receive the benefit. If the times are not settled before next August, I certainly will then leave this land of tyranny and seek a land of liberty. But for a man here to promise himself a single day to live would be presumption, for nothing but God can save us from what every Irishman must and will shortly endeavour to crush to the earth as they do us.[20]

III

By this time, Lord Edward Fitzgerald and Samuel Neilson had finally perfected their plan to seize power by insurrection. It involved three distinct phases.[21] The first would involve seizing Dublin City from within (to avoid the alarm caused by moving rural rebels into the metropolis); the key targets would be Dublin Castle, the Bank of Ireland, the Customs House and Trinity College. A second phase would mobilise the immediate crescent around the city (involving counties

Dublin, Meath, Kildare and Wicklow), whose task would be to prevent reinforcements reaching the city (especially from Loughlinstown camp). A third phase (detonated by the mail coach signal) would involve an outer tier of counties (Westmeath, Laois, Carlow, Wexford), rising a day after and preventing troop reinforcements to Dublin from any of the big camps elsewhere – like Ardfinnan and Blaris Moor. The date was set for 23 May and all was proceeding smoothly until the devastating arrest of Lord Edward Fitzgerald on 19 May. This precipitated infighting between the Sheares brothers and Neilson, and despite Neilson's best efforts, the night of 23 May failed to produce a decisive strike in the city – although the inner crescent from Dalkey to Tallaght and Lucan to Clontarf did turn out, and although the first tier counties (Meath, Kildare, Wicklow) all did mobilise as planned. The failure of the Dublin city plan, however, gave the rebellion an improvised, incoherent appearance allowing contemporaries and later historians to dismiss its levels of planning and execution.

Wexford watched and waited anxiously for news that Dublin had risen successfully. On 26 May, small groups of men were already gathering – in response to news filtering through that the midlands had risen.[22] On that Saturday, for example, the Kilcormick men were assembled by Father John Murphy under cover of a turf cutting meitheal. The actual command to rise may have been transmitted by John Hay – ironically accompanying a shaken Bishop Caulfield on the Dublin mailcoach. When it arrived in Oulart, a big crowd had already assembled – allegedly to surrender arms. While Caulfield once more harangued them, Hay slipped around the edge of the crowd, telling people to go home and hold on to their weapons: he presumably passed the order to rise to key United Irish activists in the area, because, by evening, the parish units were mobilising in the area from Bunclody to Blackwater. At six o'clock that evening, the first incident occurred at Tincurry near Scarawalsh, quickly followed by the famous incident at the Harrow.

As the hot summer night fell, the heather was blazing to indicate the gathering points, and the units converged on the two pre-assigned gathering points – at Kilthomas Hill to the north and Oulart Hill to the south. The rebels mobilised by parish in groups of around 30 to 50. The Boolavogue-Castlebridge area gravitated to Oulart Hill, while the Kilrush-Camolin area went to Kilthomas. The leadership structure at this parish level was still intact and functioning.[23] The Oulart Hill gathering had been assembled by a plethora of strong farm families – Sinnotts, Roches, Dixons, Etchinghams, Redmonds, Donovans and Dorans.[24]

The United Irish rebellion, then, in Wexford was not spontaneous or chaotic: neither did it emerge out of agrarian or sectarian issues. Instead it issued from politicisation, the spread of the United Irish movement and the deliberate creation of a mass-revolutionary policy. It was the strength of this organisation and its ability to deliver the victory at Oulart Hill that determined the success of the Wexford rising. This initial success, unlike the crushing defeats that their Meath, Kildare, Wicklow and Carlow colleagues met, determined the successful course of the rising in Wexford.

Unlike Kilthomas Hill, where panic-stricken rebels broke and ran, making easy targets for the cavalry, the Oulart Hill men held their nerve and positions – to such an extent that they were easily able to outmanoeuvre an overconfident adversary. The annihilation of 106 North Cork militia was a stunning achievement by non-professional fighting men, especially as that unit had such an unsavoury reputation. Oulart Hill lit a fire which crackled through North Wexford, igniting the insurrection in a series of rapid victories which gave them control of almost the entire county. As the campaign developed, competent leaders like Thomas Cloney and John Kelly were emerging to replace the more timid 'moderate' leadership of Bagenal Harvey and Edward Fitzgerald. In the early days of the rising, the United Irishmen's command structure had been in disarray due to the arrest of Anthony Perry (flushed out by Hardy's extreme measures across the county border). Under excruciating torture, Perry had revealed the names of Harvey, Fitzgerald and John Henry Colclough as fellow conspirators – leading to their arrests on the eve of the insurrection.

As a result, in the crucial first few days, Father John Murphy had achieved dominance in the field as a leader – although he was not an accredited United Irish leader. His success and popular acclaim made it difficult to replace him even when Harvey and Fitzgerald were released. The arguments and compromises over leadership contributed to the immobilising of the campaign after its initial energetic push; that immobility – also predicated on the sense that the United Irishmen had achieved their set task of liberating their own county – deprived them of the advantage of surprise and self confidence which had buoyed them up in their early triumphs. The Harvey/Fitzgerald leadership was also to make some poor strategic choices: Miles Byrne was suitably scathing about their preference for strategic fixed battles, which accentuated their difficulties with ammunition, ordinance and provisions.[25]

Byrne highly praised the second level of leadership – Murphy, Kelly, Cloney, Esmond Kyan, Matthew Doyle – as achieving astonishing successes with neophyte soldiers. They also showed a propensity to learn lessons quickly – becoming an increasingly formidable fighting force as time went by. Indeed, in what was to be the last major field war in

Ireland, the United Irish army maintained a campaign of great mobility across south Leinster, leading Castlereagh to warn the Chief Secretary Thomas Pelham:

> I understand ... you are rather inclined to hold the Insurrection cheaply. Rely upon it, there never was in any country so formidable an effort on the part of the people.[26]

Not just military but politically, the United Irishmen in Wexford achieved a striking success in the short-lived Wexford Republic which administered the county during the rebel occupation.[27] It was controlled by an eight-man Directory of four Protestants and four Catholics; Matthew Keugh, Bagenal Harvey, William Hatton and Nicholas Grey, and Edward Hay, Robert Meyler, Robert Carthy and William Kearney. The second tier of control – the middle management – consisted essentially of the Catholic merchants of the town, especially those radicalised in the 1790s and part of the generation schooled in the *Rights of Man* and conscious of their exclusion from the monolithically Protestant corporation – men like Edward Frayne (the £300 a year tanner), John Herron (grocer and chandler), John Murphy (hardware shopowner), Patrick Prendergast (maltster and merchant), John Scallan (sloop owner), Edward Sutton (merchant) and John Howlin (ex-American privateer and sloop owner). To bolster this experiment in representative and pluralist government, a Senate of 500 was established comprising leading citizens in the county including two representatives from each parish. The Senate was established to represent the broad popular support for the new Republic and to administer the county under the existing wartime conditions.

Their very real achievement in maintaining order in the town over the three weeks has been obscured by an event which illustrated what happened when their control was terminated – the macabre denouement of the Wexford bridge massacre. The town was remarkably well disciplined for the duration of the Wexford Republic. The committee of public safety, the passwords, the printed proclamations, the rationing arrangements, the district committees, the rebel navy – all these were substantial achievements in the turbulent hurly-burly of a fully fledged rebellion. More than any other episode in the 1798 rebellion, they mark a close parallel to the experience of the French Revolution – and a tantalising brief glimpse of the potential had there been a successful United Irish coup in Ireland.

IV

The United Irish army has been frequently dismissed as a rabble, an aimless mass of frightened, foolish or vindictive peasants. A closer examination dispels this facile and unhelpful view. The United Irish corps were created around neighbourhood or village networks of the type described by Anthony Perry: many grew out of hurling teams, mayboy groups, turf-cutting and hay-gathering meitheals, and other groups of young adult males. The fighting men were overwhelmingly young – teenagers and twenty-somethings, usually unmarried and with close ties. At the camps, Miles Byrne noted how 'the sweet cry of the name of their native barony or village roused them at once' and there is a striking vignette in Billy Byrne's trial of his corps arriving at the Gorey Hill camp, chanting 'Ballymanus, Ballymanus' as they marched.[28] Only these pre-existing linkages kept together non-professional soldiers through an arduous and exceptionally mobile military campaign. Miles Byrne praised the constancy of the rank-and-file (even under unaccustomed heavy fire) and the loyalty and cohesion of the rebel units. In this setting too, the inherited leadership role of locally potent families was important. Because young men from such families were often interrelated, kinship ties were a cementing influence on the United Irish leadership.[29]

Nor should the commitment of these men to their chosen cause be underestimated. Even their adversaries were astonished by the integrity with which they met death. The Revd Thomas Handcock talked of his hanging victims; 'almost all died with a firmness and serenity worthy of a more worthy cause'.[30] In the diary of Elizabeth Richards, there is an account of Patrick O'Brien, the schoolmaster from Piercestown. Richards relayed news of the rebel defeat at Vinegar Hill to him, commenting that 'we shall now have the blessings of peace restored'. His striking response was 'Yes', with a smile of agony and indignation, 'there will be peace but we shall all be slaves'. Even tombstones of fallen rebels could carry the message – as in his brother's epitaph for Thomas Cullen of Ballyvaldon who fell in the Battle of Enniscorthy:

> He died a victim to oppressor's rage
> Freedom his banner, liberty his badge
> Orderly United, for fight designed
> To conquer or die was well resigned

It is instructive to compare those sentiments with Thomas Pakenham's blanket judgement that 'the disaffected had no serious political aims'.

Nor should we underestimate the United Irishmen's military capabilities. Certainly, their opponents often complimented them. At the Battle of New Ross, Colonel Robert Crawfurd noted that 'I never saw troops attack with more enthusiasm than the rebels did'.[31] Miles Byrne was full of admiration for the way in which Matthew Doyle of Pollahoney (near Arklow) deployed his charges:

> I could not help admiring the clever military manner he kept his men manoeuvring, marching and counter-marching in the presence of the enemy. Doyle was stript, in his shirt, a red girdle or sash around his waist, an immense drawn sabre in his hand. He was at the head of about two hundred fine fellows, all keeping their ranks as if they had been trained soldiers and strictly executing his command.[32]

Byrne's testimony is invaluable, as Bartlett notes, because it is that of a veteran insurgent, with the immediacy of an eye-witness but with the dispassionate perspective created by distance in space and time, and by his extensive field experience in the French army, in which he rose to the level of colonel.[33]

He judged the pike to be 'a powerful weapon', especially when wielded in the intimacy of the fields, which levelled out the technological difference between the United Irish and the loyalist army. Certainly, cavalry consistently proved ineffectual against them in the *bocage* countryside of Wexford – and especially on steep hill slopes with uneven surfaces and impeded lines of vision (as at Oulart Hill). Everywhere the United Irishmen were able to get their pikemen into action at close quarters, they proved to be a formidable fighting force. Indeed, it was only when the pikemen could not engage that the rebels were impotent, as under long range artillery assault at Vinegar Hill. It was for this reason that Miles Byrne and others favoured *la petite guerre* – a guerrilla war of the flea, in which the rebels would use their superior mobility and knowledge of the hilly terrain of North Wexford and Wicklow to stay in the field until the French could land to support them. The subsequent success of Michael Dwyer in precisely this type of campaign was an example of what even a handful of determined men could achieve: as the 1798 campaign progressed, the United Irishmen showed an ability to absorb military lessons quickly.

The supposed indiscipline of the United Irish army is also open to question. The horrific massacres of Scullabogue and Wexford Bridge were two occasions when that discipline broke down and were not policy decisions by the leadership who bitterly regretted them. Edward Roche's proclamation of 7 June makes this explicit:

> In the moment of triumph, my countrymen, let not your victories
> be tarnished with any wanton act of cruelty: many of those unfor-
> tunate men now in prison were not your enemies from principle;
> most of them, compelled by necessity, were obliged to oppose
> you: neither let a difference in religious sentiments cause a differ-
> ence among the people.[34]

The rebel massacres were sharply distinguished by Byrne from the
equally horrific loyalist atrocities – which were sanctioned and commended by their leadership, right to the highest level of government. On
the issue of rape, the United Irish army occupied the high moral ground.
Their leaders constantly warned against attacks on non-combatants,
including every woman, no matter what the status of her husband. There
is no parallel on the rebel side to the routine rape inflicted by the loyalists – as, for example, the sickening multiple rapes of camp followers at
Vinegar Hill, perpetrated by the Dumbartonshire regiment, and callously
described by Archibald MacClaren in his account of the Battle. Indeed, it
was the same camp-followers who also constituted the bulk of the dead
at Vinegar Hill – killed in cold blood after the fighting men had long
retreated south via Needham's Gap. The overall casualty figures – however we estimate them – clearly demonstrate where the balance of vio-
lence lay. Of 20,000 casualties nationwide, a maximum of 3,000 were
inflicted by the rebels. Miles Byrne subsequently argued that the United
Irishmen were too gentlemanly in their warfare, too willing to rely on
negotiation, protections and non-existent government good faith. He
suggested, for example, that a mutilated rather than a cosseted
Kingsborough would have made better sense. In his view, the United
Irishmen were too squeamish when it came to the conduct of war – a
failing of which their enemies could never be accused.

Byrne also attacked those who dismissed the rebellion on account of
its sectarian dimension; because of the sectarian nature of the eighteenth-
century Irish state, any challenge to it could inevitably be interpreted by
conservatives as having a sectarian basis. The nature of eighteenth-century Irish society ensured that sectarianism is inevitably a major contextual
factor, but the rebellion itself is stripped of meaning if it is reduced to
this one issue. The sectarian model cannot explain why other equally sectarianised counties (in south Ulster and north Leinster) did not burst out
into open rebellion.[35]

In the Wexford context, the United Irishmen (whose leadership structure included at least twenty Protestants) sought to make sure that rebellion did not degenerate into an anti-Protestant pogrom. A very clear dis-

tinction was observed between loyalists (politically-active Protestants, who had joined the yeomanry or Orange Order) and neutrals (like the Quakers, or liberal Protestants like the Richards brothers, Ebenezer Jacob, etc.). Edward Roche's proclamation after the United Irishmen had taken Wexford town explicitly promised 'to protect the persons and properties of those of all religious persuasions who have not oppressed us'.[36] Women and children were respected as non-combatants: the only dereliction from this standard came with the massive breakdown of discipline which led to the Scullabogue massacre – whose victims included some wives and children of the North Cork militia.

In the wider context, contemporary commentators frequently commented that so called sectarian issues were in fact political ones. Judge Robert Day noted: 'it is only in the counties where political adventurers place themselves at the head of those sects respectively and make religion a stalking horse for electioneering purposes that these sanguinary and atrocious crimes have been committed *for the love of God!*'[37] Explaining the Armagh disturbances, one well-informed conservative offered this compellingly political argument:

> I have asserted that religion has nothing to do directly with the tumults and animosities in the county of Armagh and consequently that Orange Men are unjustly branded and for inflammatory purposes with the appellation of Bigot and Persecutor. Religion and its attachments are not warmer now in the breasts of Protestants than they were 40 years ago; yet however severe the laws then were, the people were not persecutors. To what other cause then are we to attribute the present hostility of the Protestant against the R. Catholic? 40 years ago there were no Defenders – no R.C. committees – no Conventions – no insulting and dangerous demands of Protestant property and political power, and yet the present times have been much more indulgent to the R. Caths. But I firmly believe there has not existed a single religious party in this country for above twenty years. Our parties are all purely political so that when the terms Protestant, Dissenting, or Roman Catholic interest are used, the meaning is that the person using it wishes to have, or to be supposed to have, that interest to support the point he is pressing, whatever it may be.[38]

As with sectarianism, it is equally reductionist to root the 1798 rebellion in a purely agrarian context as a kind of delayed Whiteboyism. The peasant model of late eighteenth-century Ireland envisages an artificially homogenous rural community, tarring the various strata in Irish society and their complex articulations with a simplistic brush. Miles Byrne attacked this notion, witheringly dismissing those who saw the rebellion as 'a mere revolt of ignorant, wretched peasants'. If one looks more care-fully at the Wexford situation, the sectarian and peasant solutions do not fit the complex picture. These arguments, as presented in the existing lit-erature, fail to explain why the most sectarianised (Armagh), the most class-riven (Tipperary) and the poorest (western) counties in Ireland were hardly involved in the 1798 rebellion. A broader picture stressing politicisation is crucial to understanding the causes and consequences of the rebellion.

This broad, complex picture is missing in the crude reductionism of Pakenham's *Year of Liberty*. To say, as he does, that 1798 was 'the old agrarian war under a new name', that the rebels were 'a half-disciplined mob with little idea beyond plunder', that 1798 represented merely 'the primitive forces of the countryside' is to ignore the political meaning of the 1790s, and to distort the interpretation of the rebellion itself. All the recent scholarship undermines the conventional interpretation of the rebellion as disorganised and spontaneous, with innocent 'peasants' goaded into rebellion by provocation.[39] And more recent work emphasis-es that the rebel army was not savage, cruel or vindictive, but disciplined and politically aware. Why then has the Wexford rising in particular been so often subject to this reductive interpretation? Answering this question involves exploration of the complex historiography of 1798.

V

What happened after '98 is equally important to what happened during it.[40] The rebellion immediately became a political football, endlessly kicked about during the interminable Union debates. Writing in the shadow of that debate, early commentators were either pro- or anti-Union. If pro-Union, they tended to softpedal on the issue of Catholic and United Irish culpability for the rebellion, stressing instead the provocation of the loyalists and Orange Order.[41] Anti-Unionists (the die-hard loyalist faction) stressed instead the 'popish plot' interpretation, seeing the rebellion as the third in the triptych of 1641, 1690 and 1798.

The propaganda war which ensued after 1798 ensured that the real principles of the 1790s were buried in a welter of recrimination and political point-scoring. In the acrimonious and anxious aftermath of 1798 and the Act of Union, control of the interpretation of the Rebellion became a vital component of many political agendas. Considerable energy was invested in portraying the 1798 Rebellion as a mere sectarian and agrarian revolt of ignorant Catholic peasants, in an effort to detach Presbyterians from the emerging democratic movement. This viewpoint is essentially a product of post-Rebellion propaganda, which suited both the government (anxious to diminish the threat of radical politics, and to detach the Ulster Presbyterians from their anti-establishment stance), and the United Irishmen (who were keen to distance themselves from culpability for organising a bloody armed insurrection).

The Presbyterian radical James Hope later commented on the extent of these distortions, even by former colleagues:

> It is hard for a man who did not live at the time, to believe or comprehend the extent to which misrepresentations were carried at the close of our struggle; for, besides the paid agents, the men who flinched and fell away from our cause, grasped at any apology for their own delinquency.[42]

By bitter experience, Hope understood the import of the proverb 'victory has a thousand fathers but defeat is an orphan'. In a damage-limitation exercise, the less radical wing of the United Irishmen played down their role in organising the rebellion (as in the evasive, apologetic accounts of Edward Hay, Thomas Cloney, Joseph Holt and William Farrell). This initial phase of misleading writing about the rebellion lasted until after Catholic Emancipation has been safely achieved.

By the 1840s, a second phase of writing began, which was much more explicit in acknowledging the revolutionary and republican principles of the United Irishmen, and their crucial role in organising the rebellion. This was evident in the writings of R.R. Madden, Thomas Davis (the crucial populariser of Wolfe Tone) and Luke Cullen and reached its apogee in 1863, in the *Memoirs* of Miles Byrne, the last by an active participant in the events of 1798. Byrne's candid, forceful account of the United Irishmen in Wexford became a revered Fenian text – and a problem for the institutional Catholic Church. Given Byrne's highlighting of the leading role of Catholic priests in an oath-bound secret society, how did the church justify its strident anti-Fenian stance? Father Patrick Kavanagh, a Wexford-born Franciscan friar, provided an elegant escape from this Fenian hook.[43]

Kavanagh developed a Catholic version of the Wexford rebellion as a crusade for faith and fatherland, devoid of United Irish influence. The rebellion itself was provoked not organised, its spread spontaneous, and its most important feature was clerical leadership – notably the heroic

role of Father John Murphy. According to Kavanagh, the United Irishmen were irrelevant to the Wexford rising, thereby trumping the Miles
Byrne/Fenian card: oath-bound secret societies were a liability; the only
genuine nationalist movement could be lead by Catholic priests, who
alone would provide selfless, dedicated leadership to the Irish people.
Kavanagh's text is written explicitly against the backdrop of the lurid
Cullenite assault on the Fenians and the obsessive clerical condemnation
of secret societies.

Appearing originally in 1870, but rapidly going through multiple edi-
tions, Kavanagh's *Popular History* salvaged the rebellion for Catholic
nationalists and dominated interpretation in the build up to the centenary of 1898. His version mirrors the Victorian rise to dominance of the
Catholic Church within Irish civil society, which also involved a rewrit-
ing 'backwards' of Irish history to fit this new status. At the time that
Kavanagh writes, the first Catholic diocesan histories appear, and other
influential clerical historians like Cardinal Patrick Moran had begun to
emerge.

Kavanagh's sectarian version (he was vice-president of the Ancient
Order of Hibernians, the Catholic equivalent of the Orange Order)
quickly became hegemonic within this climate of opinion – and so dominant within Wexford, for example, that it may literally have repressed
existing popular versions of the '98. It is this repression or clerical sani-
tising which accounts for the so-called 'silence' on '98 in the Wexford
folk memory of the twentieth century. After Kavanagh, 'the mighty
wave' of Father John Murphy swept all before it historiographically. The
selectivity of the Kavanagh version can be seen in his silence about
Bishop Caulfield, with his stinging condemnation of Murphy and the
other rebel priests as 'the faeces of the church'.[44]

It is important then, to bear in mind the constantly shifting and contested meaning of '98 after '98. This also obliges us to handle the sources
with forensic care, rather than treat them as objective texts – as do
Thomas Pakenham and R.B. McDowell. The fluctuating interpretative
trajectory of '98 is also a reminder that there is nothing new about the
recent revisionist debate in Irish history: this struggle over meaning and
value is a continuous one in any engagement with and understanding of
the past.

The standard narrative accounts of 1798 (Musgrave, Gordon, Teeling,
Hay...) have then to be seen as part of post-Rebellion polemics, not as
neutral or objective primary sources. Accordingly, historians who develop an interpretation based heavily on these accounts present a misleading
analysis. Once 1798 is looked at from the perspective of the 1790s (rather
than post-Rebellion hysteria), the whole picture changes. The sectarian

Henry Munroe, leader of the United Irish Army at Ballinahinch;
a Gillray cartoon; courtesy of Nicholas Robinson

and agrarian 'explanations' simply do not fit the complex pattern which one finds.

The recent overemphasis on sectarian, agrarian or millenarian motivations in 1790s radicalism presents severe interpretive difficulties.[45] Why is Tipperary (the premier county for agrarian secret societies in the eighteenth century) quiescent in 1798 while Wexford (a county devoid of these organisations and notable for its agrarian harmony) rebels? Why is Armagh – the scene of sectarian-based clashes in the late eighteenth century – not involved in the rebellion? If living conditions are the key variable, why are the poorest counties of the Atlantic coastline not involved in 1790s radicalism, and why does the United Irish rising occur instead in the Anglophone rich east coast strip from Antrim to Wexford? The agrarian argument cannot resolve these issues. As with Kavanagh's sectarian interpretation, the agrarian angle developed under the pressure of late nineteenth century events – notably the land question. Lecky and Froude both wrote explicitly against this backdrop – and both, in different ways, were pessimistic about the implications of the transition to peasant proprietorship. Their treatments of the 1790s, in which the land issue looms large, were heavily over-determined by their pressing contemporary concerns.

These falsifications have to be swept away before we can once more see the 1790s in their true context. In these circumstances, the task of the historian is clearly delineated by Walter Benjamin:

> Only that historian will have the gift of fanning the spark of hope
> in the past who is firmly convinced that *even the dead* will not be
> safe from the enemy if he wins and this enemy has not ceased to be
> victorious.

V

By relieving the Rebellion of its oppressive weight of misrepresentation, 1798 ceases to become divisive. The recent work on the period has begun to make 1798 available precisely in that fresh way, opening an invigorating and more generous space in which to consider it. That new opening has several important implications. Firstly, we must discard the now discredited sectarian version of '98, which was a polemical post-rebellion falsification. Secondly, we must stress the modernity of the United Irish project, its forward looking, democratic dimension, and abandon the outdated agrarian or peasant interpretation. Thirdly, we must emphasise the essential unity of the 1798 insurrection: what happened in Wexford was of a piece with what happened in Antrim and Down.

The single most important determinant of the Rebellion was mass-politicisation in the 1790s. It was politicisation which created the explosive cocktail of political, social, religious and economic forces. The reception of the ideology of revolutionary France was crucial; its primary impact was to widen and deepen pre-existing divisions within Irish political culture, between reformist and conservative elements, pushing one towards radicalism, the other towards repression as the 1790s progressed.

These interpretations need to be incorporated into the commemoration of the Bicentenary of the Rebellion. We can no longer afford to leave '98 to be claimed by one political tradition in Ireland. The Catholic-Nationalist version of '98 which dominated the centenary, 1938 and 1948 commemorations needs to be abandoned in favour of a pluralist, non-sectarian approach which more accurately reflects what the United Irishmen envisaged.

And if we are to fully re-engage with this invigorating version of the

United Irishman, we must also relinquish our obsession with the military aspects of 1798, with pikes and deaths, murder, mayhem and martyrdom. We should, instead, stress the living principles of democracy and pluralism which the United Irishmen formulated. The gory details of the campaign can only distract us from the enduring legacy of '98 – the political vision and moral choices which impelled men and women into the field in 1798. It is that political vision we need to reclaim and remember, not the physical defeat of the revolution on the bloody battlefields of '98.

And we need also, especially in Wexford, to constantly adhere to the international perspective of the United Irishmen – to link Bunker Hill, the Bastille and Boolavogue, to stress the enduring links which '98 forged with America, France and Australia. We need to constantly stress that 1798 in Wexford was not cabbage-patch skirmishes, but part of a national campaign, indelibly linked to what happened elsewhere – an Irish echo of the distant drums of the Atlantic Revolution.

The modern global reach of Irishness through the creation of the Irish diaspora was itself profoundly affected by the large-scale emigration and transportation of United Irishmen after the 1798 rebellion. Almost 500 were despatched to Australia as convicts, at least 2,000 went to America. These were often the brightest and best minds of their generation. Consider the striking contributions to American life made, for example, by William Sampson, William James MacNeven, Robert Adrian, John Daly Burk, Thomas Addis Emmet and John Binns – all United Irish émigrés.[46] They created an Irish-American leadership role in the diaspora which was subsequently empowered by the huge numbers which the devastating famine added. These United Irish émigrés were frequently attractive figures. Consider Miles Byrne in Paris, with his interest in novels, music and the poetry of Byron, Moore and Campbell, his pilgrimage to the Rousseau shrine at Erménonville, his fluent Spanish and his visits to Greek antiquities.[47] And yet, though he had long left Monaseed, Monaseed never left him and he remained a committed Wexfordman to the day of his death.

In response to this global dimension, our commemoration needs to be international and national as well as local. And in particular, we must be generous in our acknowledgement of the Ulster dimension and especially of the enormous contribution of the Presbyterian tradition, with its enlightened emphasis on justice, equality and liberty. In all these ways, we can make the Bicentenary open, inclusive and dynamic. We can make it speak to the Irish people as a whole, including our diaspora. We can use the 1790s as a vision and inspiration for the 1990s. Only recently, for example, have historians begun to recover the buried history of the embryonic Wexford Republic of June 1798.

With the defeat of the United Irish, this innovative experiment in democracy was suppressed with great brutality and obliterated from the historical record; its widespread support at all levels of Wexford society was denied in the anxious aftermath of 1798, and the revolution itself was then dismissively misrepresented as a mere peasant and sectarian event. By recovering the real history of the Wexford Republic, we reappropriate a profoundly democratic symbol, and an inspiring example of an effort to construct a representative, secular and pluralist politics on the island of Ireland. Two hundred years later, it can again serve to encourage us towards that imaginative inclusiveness which the United Irish had identified as being essential to unite Catholic, Protestant and Dissenter.

The Wexford Republic died in the crushing military defeat of 1798 but its brief existence was exemplary, a shining symbolic movement in Irish history. It is entirely appropriate, therefore, as we approach the Bicentenary, that we should now re-emphasise that exercise in representative government and direct democracy as a fitting and dynamic memorial to the ideals of the United Irishmen.

Sectarianism in the Rebellion of 1798: The Eighteenth-Century Context

Dáire Keogh

In her study of eighteenth-century Ireland, Edith Mary Johnston utilises an elegant aphorism to describe the period; 'for the elite [it was] an age of elegance, and for every section of the community an age of insecurity'.[1] The century was born from the embers of the Williamite Wars: while the Catholic Jacobites had been defeated, the Protestant community was left with a very real sense of their own insecurity. Fear became an obsession and within this context, any challenge to the authority of the Protestant State was inevitably interpreted as having a sectarian basis.

I

Raised on the lore of 1641, Irish Protestants believed they remained dangerously exposed to the threat of a renewed attack from a formidable Catholic enemy, both within and without the island. At the root of these fears lay the terms of the Treaty of Limerick which concluded the wars, but which left the defeated Catholics in a far stronger position than might have been expected. The implications were clear – Catholic strength implied Protestant weakness and there could be no accommodation of the two. The Protestant nation owed its very life to the destruction of Catholic power; as the Church of Ireland Archbishop of Dublin, William King, put it, 'either they or we must be ruined'.[2] It is against this pervasive background of fear that the penal laws must be set.

Recent historical writing has attempted to unravel the meaning and purpose of the laws.[3] However, the tendency to interpret the penal code from a solely Catholic perspective fails to appreciate the enduring insecurity of the Protestant minority. Their phobia is reflected in the Revd William Synge's – the popular preacher and later chancellor of St Patrick's cathedral, Dublin – toast in honour of King Billy delivered in 1714:

When I drink to the glorious memory of King William, I mean here is health to all those who love and honour the memory of King *William*, who when alive was the instrument of God's hand

> to deliver me and the Protestants of this Kingdom from arbitrary power, popery and slavery; and was instrumental, by the same good providence, to restore me and all *Irish* Protestants to our houses and lands.[4]

This sense of deliverance was real – as were the vivid memories of the 1641 massacre which were also revived at crucial moments to remind the minority of the unreliability of the Catholics. It is therefore difficult to look at the eighteenth century without understanding the depth of the divide between the people and the governing class – between the Catholic masses, the people of Ireland and the Protestant ruling elite which composed the political Nation owned the State.

There was, however, a further complication to this picture. By 'the Protestant ruling elite' is usually meant members of the established Church of Ireland, but this leaves the dissenters or Presbyterians out of the picture. When faced with the threat of a common Catholic enemy in the 1680s, Protestants of all shades joined ranks and temporarily abandoned their very real differences. Yet once the Protestants had secured their victory in 1690 and 1691, this unity quickly dissolved and intense rivalries between the church and kirk re-emerged. In the long term these divisions in Protestantism were to be of great significance, since it could not be guaranteed that the Presbyterians would remain hostile towards the Catholics forever.

A third factor contributed towards Protestant insecurity in the eighteenth century: Irish Protestants believed that the victory over the Jacobites had not been theirs alone. The determination of the Apprentice Boys of Derry and defiant cries of 'no surrender' were all well and good, but their plight was precarious until the British ships broke the boom and lifted the siege of the city. The lessons of the episode were all too clear: the security of Protestant Ireland ultimately depended on the British connection.

While the insecurity of the ruling class is understandable, we must not lose sight of the plight of the dispossessed majority. The penal laws may not have been as severe as was once believed – perhaps they were more of a reasonable inconvenience than a draconian code. Yet while the provisions of the laws were never fully implemented, Edmund Burke observed, 'connivance is the relaxation of slavery, not the definition of liberty'. No matter how the laws are interpreted, they psychologically isolated the majority population, creating an *ancien régime* society with its rigid distinction between the Nation and the State.

In the early decades of the century, however, there was little hope of redress for Catholic grievances. Bartlett sums up this situation:

Friars watching drownings, frontispiece (woodcut), Sir John Temple,
The Irish Rebellion, 6th ed. (Dublin 1724)

So long as Protestant unity lasted, so long as a good relationship
existed between successive British governments and the Irish
Parliament, so long as the political elite of both countries saw eye
to eye on the menace of popery, there would be no prospect of
movement on the Catholic Question.[5]

II

The complex unfurling of the eighteenth century, however, dismantled
these safeguards. By the 1780s the term 'Protestant Ascendancy',
described not a united and confident ruling elite, but rather a beleaguered
minority. The arrogant posturing of the Protestant Patriots and
Volunteers had strained the Anglo-Irish relationship. Loyalty had been
the Catholic trump card since the 1760s. In the period 1778-82, the
Catholic community began to appear as an attractive potential ally for
the government in the face of insistent Volunteer demands for free trade
and legislative independence.

In this context, the limited Catholic relief measures conceded in this
period could be interpreted as an implicit attempt by the Government to

woo their support. Alternatively it has been suggested that the British government was attempting to call the Protestants to their senses by playing the Catholic card. Whatever the case, the lessons were not lost on the increasingly anxious minority: their insecurity was reinforced by the realisation that by 1791 England regarded the Ascendancy as 'only one description of Irishmen'.[6]

Events in Revolutionary France further contributed to the insecurity of the Ascendancy. The Protestant unity which had been present in the 1690s was long gone. The Protestants had divided on the issue of parliamentary reform and Catholic relief in the 1780s. The *ancien régime* was based on the acceptance of inequality; French revolutionary principles insisted on the essential equality of all men. Any concession in this direction would strike at the very foundations of Ascendancy.

This in itself was a significant development; equally significant was the real fear that Presbyterians and Catholics would join ranks in a political conspiracy. In the eighteenth century, Catholicism had been identified with arbitrary government – as Sir Edward Newenham M.P. put it, 'we are for freedom, they are for despotism'.[7] Events in France, however, had altered perceptions. Not only were Catholics capable of living in freedom, but they had overthrown the regime in the 'eldest daughter of the church' and the French now basked in a liberty more advanced than that delivered to the British by the Glorious Revolution of the previous century.

The collapse of parliamentary reform in the 1780s on the question of Catholic relief illustrated that no reform movement could be successful unless it addressed the Catholic question. Tone's *Argument on behalf of the Catholics of Ireland* sought to bring this point home to Ulster Presbyterians in the conviction that, as Burrowes had argued six years earlier, the Catholics also 'live in a period of liberation – and [have] caught the love of freedom from yourselves'.[8]

Tone's polemic paved the way for Presbyterian and Catholic radicalism to come together in the formation of the United Irishmen in late 1791. Nevertheless, a significant segment of Presbyterian opinion remained to be convinced of this sudden transformation in its ancient enemy and sectarianism continued to impede popular union. The implications of such an alliance for the Ascendancy were enormous, but the existence of sectarian tensions provided one possible key to its defeat. If these could be exploited, the 'union of affection' could be sundered and rendered impotent.

In an effort to prevent this 'uniting business' between the Presbyterians and Catholics, the Ascendancy actively promoted the religious animosity which the radicals had sought to eliminate. Tone hoped to

'United Irishmen in training': a Gillray cartoon published in June 1798;
courtesy of Nicholas Robinson

unite 'Catholic, Protestant and Dissenter under the common name of Irishmen', but the Armagh priest, James Coigley believed that it was 'of great utility to the Irish government that such religious disputes should exist between Dissenters and Catholics'.[9]

Coigley embarked on missions to the Presbyterians of Antrim and Down in an effort to convince them of Catholic good intentions. In this context, too, the Presbyterian radical, the Revd William Steel Dickson, dismissed by loyalists as 'a papist at heart', addressed a sermon to a congregation at Portaferry on Christmas Day 1792 in which he condemned the 'malicious whisperer's artful tale ... the base insinuations of the crying sycophant, and the false representations of the officious partisan'.[10]

The timing of Steel Dickson's address was significant. December 1792 saw the meeting of the celebrated Catholic Convention in Tailors' Hall – the great representative assembly styled the 'Back Lane Parliament' by its loyalist critics. United Irishmen had played a key role in this meeting. This alarmed Protestant sensitivities, which were inflamed by the Convention's decision to appeal directly to the King over the head of the viceroy. This was seen as a grievous affront to the Irish establishment which spoke volumes about Catholic intentions. However, under pressure from London, the Irish parliament was forced to concede the 40s. franchise to the Catholics in 1793.

Two Cruikshank cartoons; (above) a loyalist interpretation of the
massacre on Wexford bridge; (below) Father Murphy and the
'heretic bullets'

The rapid pace of events in the country increased Protestant paranoia and the sense that a popish plot was once more a foot. The advent of war with France in February 1793, however, altered the attitude of the British government towards Ireland. This was no time for further constitutional experimentation and the government consciously encouraged the loyalist faction. The Relief Act of 1793 was accompanied by an unpopular militia bill which robbed it of its popularity. This gross affront to Catholics was followed by a Convention Act, outlawing political assemblies, which effectively ended the open campaigning of the Catholic Committee and United Irishmen.

The short viceroyalty of the pro-Catholic and liberal minded Earl Fitzwilliam in 1795 revived Catholic hopes for full emancipation. However, the Viceroy's hasty dismissal of the anti-Catholic Castle troika of John Beresford, Arthur Wolfe and Edward Cooke resulted in his recall. The reinstatement of the junta renewed loyalist confidence and the new viceroy, Earl Camden, arrived with specific instructions to 'rally the Protestants'. St Patrick's College Maynooth was established in a final effort to calm Catholic grievances. It was to be a bone for the dogs, or a sop for the loss of emancipation; even more than this, it was a cynical and successful attempt to dissuade the hierarchy from any flirtation with Catholic out of doors politics.[11]

According to Thomas Hussey, the College's first president, the country was on 'the brink of civil war'.[12] The United Irishmen had been driven underground, but their advanced leadership pursued a plan for rebellion with French assistance. They had formed important links with the dormant Catholic Committee and had absorbed the Defender organisation of South Ulster. This was a radical alliance, one which embraced many political and religious persuasions, but loyalist opinion continued to characterise it in sectarian terms as a popish plot. Any other interpretation of such spectacular disturbances, implied that the regime needed reformation, a step not possible without the elite surrendering their cherished ascendancy.

The establishment rallied to the banner of the Protestant Ascendancy. The foundation of the Orange Order in 1795 appealed to the sectarian memory of 1641 – the very memories the United Irishmen had sought to erase.[13] James Hope, the Presbyterian radical dismissed the Order as:

> a faction of intolerant, turbulent men ... persecuting yeomen, renegade 'croppies', the hangers-on about landlords, and low-church clergymen with their spies and informers, all over the country ... the bullies of certain houses in garrison towns, and those of fairs and markets in rural districts.[14]

At first the authorities in Dublin and London were sceptical about the Order, but in time as law and order broke down they came to regard this lawless faction as a vital weapon in their armoury in the fight against rebellion. As Thomas Knox, the military commander in Ulster, put it to Edward Cooke in August 1796:

> We must to a certain degree uphold them, for with all their licentiousness, on them we must rely for the preservation of our lives and properties should critical times occur.[15]

A month later, the loyalist *Dublin Journal*, dismissed rumours concerning the Orange Order. Orangemen, the paper stated, 'declare no bigotry or fanaticism, or illiberal prejudice', but were 'willing to live in harmony' with Turk, Jew, Arab, Cherokee, 'even the Arch Devil himself ... provided the latter gentleman will behave himself properly, find security that he will cut no caper among them in the shape of a Defender, or an United Irishman'.[16]

Orangemen enlisted en masse in the new Yeomanry Corps and a blind eye was turned to the terror they inflicted in the north, which James Coigley compared to the 'tyranny of Robespierre'.[17] In the House of Commons, James Verner, referring to the reports of 7,000 Catholics been driven from Ulster in fear of their lives, cynically declared 'whatever the Roman Catholics have suffered they have brought upon themselves'.[18] On the other side of the coin, the Orange bogey became an effective part of the United Irish propaganda machine and fabricated Orange Oaths to massacre Catholics were published in the radical *Press* (October, 1797).

III

The final burst of Rebellion in May 1798 came as a relief to the government. The winter of 1797-8 witnessed the spread of chronic disaffection beyond Ulster into much of Leinster and parts of Connacht and Munster. The draconian methods employed by the government – even Lake's brutal dragooning of Ulster had failed, so the government welcomed the eventual eruption as an opportunity to declare full scale war on what had been a frustratingly hidden conspiracy.

It is in this sense that Edward Cooke hailed the outbreak as 'the salvation of the country'. Yet in the early stages of the rebellion, it appeared as if the United Irish rebels were to be the saviours.[19] By 5 June it was the cabinet's unanimous opinion that without the arrival of a large army from England 'the kingdom is gone'.[20]

Loyalist correspondence and reports abounded in lurid tales of atrocities and these were inevitably given a sectarian hue. 'Inevitably' because the state itself was Protestant – and because the loyalists had consciously defined themselves as the 'Protestant Ascendancy' since the 1780s in the face of rising challenge from liberal Protestants and the papist majority. The radical inspiration of the rebellion was ignored. French principles and the United Irish reform programme were dismissed as simply a 'popish plot'.

Certainly the rebellion provided an opportunity to settle old scores, particularly in Wexford where the county had been bitterly divided on the question of parliamentary reform. Lord Shannon's report on the condition of Wexford in June 1798 reflected loyalist paranoia:

> One [Ebenezer] Jacob of Wexford, a Protestant, has been made chief magistrate by the rebels, which is a matter of much surprise. He has saved Kingsborough's [commander of hated North Cork militia] life, though it is said, but I don't believe it, that they flogged him and asked him how he liked *that*.[21]

The massacres, too, have been given subjective analysis. The events on Wexford Bridge awoke horrific memories of 1641. The burning of the barn at Scullabogue is represented as a sectarian outrage, but there is no mention in Musgrave of the unprovoked massacre of 28 prisoners by the yeomen in the ball alley at Carnew.[22] Again, attacks by the rebels on Protestant clergymen are described as sectarian acts, overlooking the fact that many of their number were magistrates who had forcibly upheld a tyrannical regime. The atrocities of the government forces are excused, while the rebel armies are summarily dismissed as 'drunkards, robbers and cannibals'.[23] There is no doubt that during the rebellion both parties exploited sectarian fears – there are the embarrassing examples of conversions and baptisms – but these were secondary to the trust of the rebellion; the Scullabogue and Wexford Bridge events occurred when the United Irish discipline broke down, not when it was in place.[24]

IV

It was convenient for the ultras to interpret the rising in this simplistic sectarian fashion: many were only too eager to accept George Taylor's observation that 'none of the rebels were so blood-thirsty, as those who were most regular attendants at the popish ordinances'.[25] Musgrave's *Memoirs of the Rebellion*, are teeming with bizarre examples of Catholic

A Cruikshank cartoon depicting the rebels carousing in the palace of the
Church of Ireland bishop of Ferns

excesses, the purpose of which was to illustrate their unreliability. The
events of 1798 had shown them as incapable of liberty. Security, he
argued, lay in Protestant unity – this was the lesson of 1641, 1690 and
1798. It was time for the Presbyterians to end their *liason dangereuse*
with French principles. It is, however, essential to bear in mind that
Musgrave's *Memoirs* became, what Dickson has called 'the political bible
for a party, not the whole Protestant community'.[26]

The liberal protestant reformers and Catholics had been compromised by the rebellion and in the subsequent polemic they were anxious
to distance themselves from any conspiracy. It was this preoccupation
which explains the willingness of many apologists, Edward Hay and
company, to stress the sectarian aspect of the rebellion in an effort to
minimise attention on reformers, the Catholic Committee and the
United Irishmen. The Catholic clergy, too, had been compromised and
the hierarchy embarked on a policy of damage limitation, representing
the active clerics as 'giddy' unreliable characters. In this scenario, Father
Murphy and his colleagues were no heroes, but were described by their
bishops as 'the very faeces of the church'.[27]

The complicated issues of the century re-emerged in the Union
debate. Ironically, the ultras were the strongest opponents of the mea-

sure. The Union would end any pretence of the Protestant Irish Nation, but more than that it would open the door to Catholic emancipation. On the other hand, liberal Protestants sponsored the project of a union, precisely because it offered the prospect of reform. The Catholic hierarchy gave their assent to the union because Pitt had implied a promise of emancipation, but Bishop Hussey of Waterford put it more bluntly, declaring preference for a union with 'the Beys and Mamelukes of Egypt to that of being under the iron rod of the Mamelukes of Ireland'.[28]

This was the great irony of the 1790s that the decade which began with the hopes of a republic and a brotherhood of affection ended with war and the subsequent Act of Union. But Union without emancipation contained a fatal flaw which eventually transformed the Catholic question into the Irish question.[29]

The United Irishmen in Wexford

L.M. Cullen

The significance of the 1790s in Ireland may be compared to Revolution in France. In both countries events raised profound issues which are central to human experience. The dramatic events of the period brought not only changes to social and political life, but personal triumph and tragedy. Moreover, the decade raised universal issues which every age interprets anew. In this sense there is no all-embracing assessment of events, nor a stable perception of their meaning or message.

I

In subsequent generations, the concepts and phrases of the 1790s acquired a simplified meaning which falsified the realities of the decade. The yeomen, for example, were seen as terrorists who ill-treated the people and drove them into rebellion. This view of yeomen as Protestant fanatics is taken for granted even to-day in Nancy Curtin's quite excellent *The United Irishmen* (Oxford, 1994). The reality however is quite different. Many of the yeomen – a form of territorial force raised by individual gentry who held official commissions for the purpose – were Catholic. Moreover, in contrast to the militia where Catholic officers were rare, there were many Catholic yeomanry officers. Included in this number was Edward Roche, a member of Le Hunte's yeoman at Castlebridge, who joined the rebellion in his regimental uniform.

When the yeomanry was created in 1796 the United Irishmen debated whether they should join. In the south it was quickly decided to join, but in the north this response was slower and less universal. Moreover, the government was powerless to exclude Catholics from the officer ranks as they had done with the militia. Since the formation of yeomen units depended upon local circumstances, prominent liberals as well as conservatives recruited units. Liberals regularly appointed Catholic officers, while some units had a majority of Catholics in the rank and file.

At the outset of 1798, a campaign began in Wicklow, Kildare and Wexford to force the liberal gentry to eject Catholics from their units as suspected United Irishmen. In many cases, and in all three counties, the leaders of yeomanry corps resisted this pressure. Thus the real story of

A loyalist caricature of the United Irish alliance with the French;
courtesy of Nicholas Robinson

the yeoman is not about the persecution of the population, but rather of
a political struggle in which the liberal gentry with some success resisted
this pressure to eject Catholics. In some cases units were disbanded precisely because of the unwavering liberal sentiments of their leaders. Some
had a complex story like Hume's, Saunders', and Edwards' in Wicklow,
but in Wexford there were similar units including Le Hunte's.

II

Yet the story which has persisted is of a Catholic rebellion in Wexford,
which began as a response to oppression and was led by priests. If this
was so, and if the 'reluctant' lay leaders in the rising were acquired by
intimidation from propertied Catholics, the rebellion in the county
would have been different from elsewhere. It would also seem peculiar

that, without organisation, such large numbers, motivated simply by fear, were able to conduct a three-week campaign in an area covering two-thirds of the county.

Nevertheless, this version of events, which was repeated in the last three decades the nineteenth century, became the orthodoxy of the twentieth century. It derived from two circumstances; the growing prominence of the Irish Church and the struggle between the Church and the Fenians, whose scale and persistence we must not underestimate. Heavily influenced by Rome's anxiety to secure the political power of the Church amongst the laity, the clergy sought not simply to lead Irish Catholics but, as home rule seemed likely to materialise, to dominate Irish society at large. Accordingly, history was rewritten and in a sense taken over.

The struggle with the Fenians over the legacy of 1798 began as early as 1870 in Kavanagh's *History* or perhaps in 1877 when the Fenians were prevented from placing their first monument on their chosen site.[1] When the 1898 celebrations took place, the initiative came from the Fenians (or their successors the IRB). However, in a real sense, while the Fenians organised the events, the Churchmen and the Irish parliamentary party politicians moved in on the movement. The Fenians did the organising, and the Churchmen and the politicians commanded the rhetoric.

III

This late nineteenth century interpretation of 1798 is an interesting instance of how the understanding of events changed over time and is the last of three stages in the unfolding of the story of the great year itself. During the first of the three phases, from 1798 to 1838, the events of '98 were played down. This resulted, in part, from an effort to rebut exaggerated loyalist accounts in order to facilitate the final step in Catholic emancipation. It was also due to practical considerations, as participants sought to play down their role in 1798.

These practical reasons were pressing. Initially there was the urgency of making legal defence against charges which could have resulted in the loss of their lives. Later, more mundane or personal reasons came to the fore. In Farrell's case it was personal justification of abandoning his comrades; in the case of Holt the priority was to ward off attention from people who wanted to revive the matter in his business life, and ultimately in the light of his business failures the prospect of making money from the publication of his memoirs.[2] Thomas Cloney had abandoned the idea of writing in the early 1800s, but wrote an account in 1832 because he

wanted to refute charges that he had burned the church at Old Ross and
could have been involved in the massacre at Scullabogue. These allega-
tions had been revived in order to prevent the renewal of the alliance of
repealers and liberal Protestants of which Cloney was an activist.[3]

The second of the three interpretative phases, beginning in the 1830s,
was one of explicit recognition of the political purpose of the rebellion.
In a curious way, this is present even in Cloney's *Narrative* which
includes both denials of United Irish membership and detailed accounts
of active service by himself and other named persons. Nevertheless,
explicit recognition became public with Madden's *United Irishmen* in
1842, and the writings of Thomas Davis who penned a glowing account
of Wexford.

This mood had a popular basis, which can be seen in the compilations
of Brother Luke Cullen.[4] The Carmelite began his writing in 1838 but,
for the most part, his manuscripts do not contain the testimony of eye
witnesses. Rather, this material was recorded from individuals who recol-
lected what people had said to them in the 1820s or later. Cullen's
enquiries were apparently prompted by the appearance of Holt's book in
1838, which failed to mention Michael Dwyer and lacked a description
of what happened in and after June 1798.

These omissions explain why Cullen began to fill in the story of
Wicklow and Wexford and why Dwyer's role, and events revolving
around the Dwyer-Holt relationship, feature so prominently in his writing. The Dwyer evidence takes up a whole volume and the mass of material explains why it was possible for Charles Dickson, a century later, to
devote a long book to Michael Dwyer.[5] Cullen's compilations extended
into an account of Garrett Byrne, socially the most prominent of the
Wicklow United Irishmen, which is both flattering and fanciful. The
accident of the availability to him of a fragment of a pamphlet by John
Edwards explains why he became aware of the events in Newtown-
mountkennedy and the role of Edwards in opposing the change in security policy from legal to illegal methods in April 1798.

Cullen's account is politically conscious and geographically selective.
While he extended his account into Wexford, the rebellion there was not
his main purpose. It was an accident of the fact that he had spent some
years of his youth in Wexford and had gone to school in Glenbrien. His
Wexford account is confined largely to the events of the Gorey-
Kilcormick-Oulart axis a few miles north and east of Glenbrien, and to
the retreat from Wexford into Wicklow and the midlands, which caught
his interest primarily because Garrett Byrne as well as the local hero of
the Kilcormick region was involved in it. Cullen has nothing to say on
west Wexford; there is no reference to Cloney, except as a relative of

Sinnott who lived near Glenbrien, none to the Bantrymen, and scarcely any to the events in Wexford town. Moreover, the most important of the clergymen, Philip Roche, is not a figure in the book, and the other clergymen, Michael Murphy, Kearns and Clinch feature little if at all and although he has some information on Esmond Kyan he admits to have known little about him.

Cullen later claimed that he had devoured Hay's *History* when it first appeared in 1803.[6] Yet, he was only ten years old at the time and, quite clearly, the issues which concerned Hay did not preoccupy Cullen in 1838. Nevertheless, Cullen's remarks are interesting because they suggest an avid interest in 1803 in the rebellion issue. Similarly, the details he gathered in 1838 or later show that memory of the rebellion was very much alive in 1820. Cullen's informants had been talking to fellow Wexfordmen about the events of 1798 and their perception of the rebellion, at least in Kilcormick, was quite different from the strange version contained in Banim's *Croppy Boy*. This was written on the premise that if emancipation was granted, there was no danger the bogeyman of 1798 would return. Contrary to what Charles Dickson suggested in his history of the Wexford rebellion, silence about it had not fallen on Wexford.[7]

Cullen is more impressive for his incidental detail than for his generalisations. The accounts of 25 and 26 May at Oulart, of Sparks and Turner, of the murder of rector Burrowes at Kyle, and of the battles are fragments which have a ring of truth, humanity and tragedy as well as realism. He did not stress the priests heavily, and in fact his sources told him that Murphy was of little help in the crucial battle of Oulart. Those who were of most effect were Edward Roche and, above all, Morgan Byrne who was later condemned and written out of history because of his alleged savagery.

Ironically, given the fact that Cullen sought to record the purpose of Wexford and Wicklow men, the subsequent use of his material has reinforced the impression that the rebellion began in a single location, that its spread was spontaneous, and that beyond a handful of locations, there was no prior story to record. The result is that, quite wrongly, Father Murphy has become the symbol of the Wexford rebellion, certainly something that Cullen did not intend. Murphy's prominence is ambivalent. His prominence is evident, but he was neither the sole nor the most effective leader; his importance lay more in the fact of his having led the first successful action of the opening night.

Yet Father Murphy's prominence had emerged before Cullen's manuscripts began to be widely used. This was mainly because Father Kavanagh, who was from the region, moved Murphy to centre stage, less

General Lake, Commander in Chief of
the crown forces in Ireland

because of his intrinsic importance than because Kavanagh centred his
account on him. In a very real sense, Kavanagh's book was written not
about priests but around Murphy on his own. The book is based on solid
knowledge; his correction of the sequence of the rebellion and chapel
burning is correct, and there is some interesting family lore.

Kavanagh's *History* illustrates that memory of 1798 was still very
much alive, and the place Father Murphy assumed in both Cullen and
Kavanagh, writing 30 years apart and with very different motives, suggests that his memory had left a very large local impact and that Bishop
Caulfield's unkind verdict may have been too readily accepted. In
Cullen's account, written earlier but widely used only later, Murphy's
status appears to be confirmed from the coincidence that his evidence
comes from the perspectives of men living in a single location and of his
detailing what happened there in the early hours of the rebellion.

Interest in the United Irishmen grew rapidly at national level with
Madden's work, published several times and in the final edition in 1860
which at last incorporated some of Cullen's Wexford information.[8]
Kavanagh's account however, was written not to build up the rebellion,
but to oppose Fenianism and to play down all hints of prior organisation. More specifically, its purpose was to rebut Miles Byrne's account,
published in 1863, which was self-consciously intended to revive political interest in the 1798 rebellion.[9] Particularly embarrassing was Byrne's
defence of the priests as political rebels, especially John Murphy whom
he knew and regarded favourably.

Kavanagh does not use Byrne's account; he is mentioned by name
only once, and then merely to say that he was too young to have an

accurate memory of the rebellion. The clergy at large are substantially written out of Kavanagh's account to concentrate on one figure, John Murphy. His status as a mere curate is ignored, as is the earlier emphasis of both the Bishop of Ferns and Edward Hay that no parish priest had been involved and that only misguided curates had taken the field.

Falsification of the story in 1870 or in 1898 means that, despite earlier evidence that a lively recollection had survived, all subsequent tradition has to be regarded with great suspicion. A distinction must be made between versions which, up to the end of the 1830s, were authentic and others from the 1870s which, though synthetic and suspect were consecrated in Patrick McCall's misleading *Boolavogue*.

IV

The role of oppression as the cause of the rising on 26 May is buttressed by presenting the massacres at Carnew, Dunlavin and Hacketstown as the ultimate catalyst of rebellion, rather than the reports of outbreaks in other parts, which seems in point of time to have arrived ahead of the other news. The fact that Cullen's informants seem to have taken this line is less a consequence of their impact than of Cullen's Wicklow perspectives. Cullen's visits to Wexford seem to have been short; he collected little if any evidence beyond his informants in the Glenbrien region, and he did not go back over the evidence in the way that he did time and time again for Wicklow.

Thus, while he allegedly read Edward Hay's account as far back as 1803, he was not so concerned to correct this work as he had been with Holt's account. Unlike his account of Wicklow, Cullen never deals explicitly with the evidence of a United Irish organisation and leadership in County Wexford. Nevertheless, since it existed, it emerges spontaneously and without any conscious effort on Cullen's part. It is evident in the role attributed to John Hay; in his account of Sparks' awaiting instructions and his intention of going to Edward Fitzgerald's. It is clear too, in Murphy's dispatch of a messenger southwards after the Harrow, and in references to the later local lore. The impression which emerges is that Cullen's informants were able to fill him in on many details, but that he did not choose for practical reasons to pursue them further.

If the absence of a political framework in Wexford has been marked, there has also been a reluctance in the literature on the 1790s throughout Ireland to allow a political role to rural rebels. Emphasis has been heavy on sectarianism, millenarianism and agrarianism as the motivating force of movements and their spread outside the towns. Thus, the Defenders in Bartlett's and Elliott's accounts are motivated by disappointment at unfulfilled expectations of relief in 1792-3 and by class war against comfortable Catholics as beneficiaries of the legal changes.[10]

Unrest however, was more complex and in 1793 and 1794 comfortable Catholics and the lower classes drew closer together rather than apart. Few well-off Catholics were given a place on the grand juries, or as Justices of the Peace, while few acceded to the commissioned ranks of the militia. For the rank and file the issue of compulsory attendance at religious services was in many but not all regiments a grievance, which became a major public one at the end of 1794. By September 1795, Edward Cooke, struggling in the Castle to understand the Defenders, had come to the conclusion that 'the better class of Roman Catholics ... seem to look with composure on transactions which might eventually involve them as well as all other descriptions of persons in ruin and destruction'.

The scale and success of the Wexford rebellion, then, has been attributed to the fact that these motives, supposedly present everywhere, were held to have been particularly strong in the county. Thus, Lecky assumed that the Wexford rising was agrarian, and Charles Dickson held also that the Defenders were exceptionally numerous and strong in Wexford.[11] However, the near-success of Wexford was due to more mundane reasons. Firstly, Wexford was the only instance where the rebellion had sustained military victories in the early days, an astonishing run from 27 May to 4 June. Secondly, the competence of the captains is crucial as is the fact that virtually none of them had been taken up before the rebellion; four of the seven or more colonels remained at liberty in the first days of the Wexford rebellion.

More important still was the role of west Wexford which in the twelve months before mid-1798 had been the slowest region of North Wexford to organise but which for that reason lacked the internal divisions between old-style moderates and radicals of east Wexford. Given an absence of more established local figures with political ambitions, youth was also on the side of the West Wexford radicals, and Cloney and Kelly were leaders of some ability. They had the largest and best organised force of all the rebel divisions and took the field in numbers in a campaign which later ground into immobility. At Ross they were with some exceptions the only force which engaged, and the replacement of Harvey by Philip Roche two to three days later reflected the divide between the two sectors of the county organisation.

Roche, Kelly and Cloney had been active in an overlapping area from Poulpeasty to Killane. I think that the conclusion may be inescapable that Kelly and Cloney were the leaders of a Bantry formation which split before the rebellion into two regiments with Kelly and Cloney the respective colonels; Roche, though Bantry-based, may have become colonel for Scarawalsh barony. Roche seems variously to have stayed at Enniscorthy and to have operated to it's north in the early days; Cloney and Kelly went from Vinegar Hill to Three Rocks and then to Ross. After Ross, Roche joined the Bantry forces, operating in the south continuously with Cloney as his main commander.

Luke Cullen's account, written from evidence of east Wexford and his interest in Byrne and Murphy, illustrates how even when the movement fell apart, it was far from homogenous: the bands that moved into Wicklow and the midlands were conspicuously an east Wexford and Wicklow force. Philip Roche's views on what to do were also different from those of the others, wiser I believe in their pessimistic appraisal of future prospects, even if not on what his fate would be riding into Wexford after its surrender.

V

If we look back at the early 1790s, we face the problem of understanding the Defenders and their aims and spread.[12] The issues raised by the Catholic question in the 1780s and early 1790s were particularly bitter in the regions of Ulster, north Leinster, and north Connaught where the Protestant presence ranged from regions with large numbers, sometimes a majority, into regions where their numbers were small. This frontier ran from south Down and Armagh through Louth, Meath, Cavan, Longford to a region embracing Leitrim and into Sligo and the border districts within Roscommon and Mayo.

Within this area, the Catholic question, which had been a live issue from 1782 onwards, took root in the Volunteer politics of Armagh, Louth, Mayo and Sligo. Hence an existing divide became particularly bitter in 1791-2, and peaks of tension centred on south Down/Louth/Armagh, and also north Roscommon and its borders where the presence of a small but articulate group of propertied Catholics helped to fan the flames.

In contrast to Wexford, whose Catholics did not feature in the early United Irishmen, a strong knot of north Connaught Catholics and a thin scatter from the Armagh border region were present in the early Dublin society of United Irishmen. They produced some of the activists of later military action such as the Carolans, and in the west the two well connected and forceful figures of Plunkett and McDonnell. Though agrarian and other complaints existed, they were not the sole issues. Moreover, they existed before the militia riots of 1793, and the wave of attacks on houses in north Connaught singled out the homes of those figures who had a hard profile on the political and Catholic questions alike. Two years later in April 1795 the killing of 11 revenue officers in Leitrim came from a general build-up of tensions, and was part of an accelerating preoccupation in the early spring by defenders and authorities alike with the area.

Likewise, we must be careful about accepting the commonly held assumption, that radical politics suffered a loss of momentum in 1793 and 1794. We know little for these years. Tone's diaries do not exist for them, and the belief that he was undecided or discouraged is not consistent with what little we know of him. In a larger sense there is scanty information, and Thomas Collins, the only worthwhile government spy at the time, was lamenting that the real subversives met outside the committee meetings. Besides, the Government itself was paralysed from July 1794 to March 1795, because of the expected and then short-lived Fitzwilliam viceroyalty. In the same period, Collins coincidentally ceased to provide information not because the United Irishmen were dissolved, but because his financial problems forced him to go into hiding from his creditors.

No intelligence network existed; the will to maintain one almost evaporated for these nine months so that it had to be built up anew in 1795 and 1796. With the collapse of the Fitzwilliam viceroyalty and the return to power of the old group in March-April 1795, litigation against subversives quickened up. The recruitment of spies began afresh, and Tone who had dallied in the country despite an undertaking in May 1794 to leave, lost no time in doing so. It is these new circumstances and the return of the old guard and their policies to Dublin Castle which explains the Leitrim confrontation of April 1795.

The basis for government action in the west stemmed from a small amount of correspondence, received principally in March-May, some of which came from army officers who had just been moved into the region. This painfully small and not always well informed corpus of letters became the source of the first digest of information about Defenders. It does not rest on wide information over a long period: it is the fruit of a small amount of information brought together in haste. A second digest was written in September in wake of the trial and execution of the Meath Defender Laurence O'Connor.[13]

This second digest is based on little perceptible increase in information. It rested largely on evidence from court cases, and one of the problems was that one of the defendants had maintained an obdurate silence. However, the O'Connor trial and a small collection of documents found

on some of the prisoners had alerted the Castle to the political framework of the Defenders who were described as 'contaminated with the
chimerical and seditious doctrines of the times ... ' and motivated by
'religious animosity and impatience of political restrictions'. The government descent into illegality began in the west in May 1795, almost immediately on the return of the old executive and while they were still grop-
ing in alarm to weigh up the wider implications of events there.

An agrarian or even sectarian framework is not obvious: in the handful of letters from 1795, all spread over a period of about three months,
agrarian unrest is referred to in only two of the letters. Thomas Russell
and Tone were also becoming upbeat about the political outlook of the
people in 1793-4. An interest by the United Irishmen in the Defender
districts stemmed back to the summer of 1792. However, a serious interest by the United Irishmen of building a systematic branch or lodge
structure for themselves began only when it became clear in the north
that the Volunteers could no longer be a vehicle of dissemination of
United Irishmen activity. The United Irishmen began to spread seriously
in cell structure outside Belfast only in the second half of 1794 and since
the Defender organisation, in evidence from as early as 1789, had preceded the United Irish organisation in the countryside, the closer ties of
1795-6 took the form of joint membership; in the language of the day,
they were either 'up' or 'up and up'. The journeys by United Irishmen to
Armagh in 1795 and much further afield by Charles Teeling were among
the first stages of this operation.

Defenders and United Irishmen alike were slow to spread in the
south. The Defenders were reaching Leitrim and Kildare in 1795, and
this explains the alarms of April and July 1795 in Dublin Castle. In the
south the United Irishmen were at first slow to spread outside Dublin.
That was in part due to a protracted divide, from May 1794 to October
1796, between ambitious barristers and their Dublin associates, who
were keen on organising the United Irishmen as a political society, and
others who wanted the Society to organise in depth in cell structure. The
advance of a subversive organisation was easier in the north, because
Belfast lacked the presence of ambitious figures, who encouraged by the
presence of the law courts and parliament, saw radical causes as a means
of orthodox political advancement rather than a means of subverting
existing political society by underground organisation. Hence, in contrast to Belfast, there was a protracted struggle in Dublin for two years
between those who wanted a comparatively open society and those who
wanted an organisation based on a cell structure.

VI

Attitudes to the French Revolution remain a key to the question of 1790s politicisation. In Wexford, one of the centres of radical action in the Catholic Convention of 1792, James Edward Devereux, knew France well, and had been present in Paris two decades earlier for the marriage of one of Sutton's daughters. Sutton, a Wexford man, close friend of England's old enemy Choiseul, was an organiser of privateering ventures against England in the early 1780s. Edward Hay had been educated abroad and was a close ally of Devereux in 1792. Harvey Hay was not opposed to Catholic assertiveness: he was very active as late as early 1795, and the divide with Edward must have arisen from the question of passing from assertiveness into Uniting politics. Edward Sweetman had served as a French officer, and William Barker, a 1798 rebel, served on the greatest of all Sutton's vessels, the *Comte d'Artois*.

How did the French Revolution affect those who had been abroad as priests or officers? A simple model is usually presented; Catholics were inherently loyal, they obeyed their superiors, they were frightened by the excesses of the Revolution and so on. However, it is not clear that either officers or priests were uniformly opposed to revolution: they divided on the issue.[14] Hence, we must be careful about assuming loyalty or believing the question to be straightforward. Our picture is coloured by the frenetic posturing of Caulfield, the bishop of Wexford, and the later campaign against the Fenians. Even Father Kavanagh, in quoting evidence from one of his ancestors, slipped into admitting that some of the priests, having tasted liberty abroad, would like it at home.

The loyalism of Archbishop Troy and Caulfield and that which they painted for Catholics, is too readily accepted at face value. In Wexford even the specific events of 25 and 26 May had a political context. Parishioners at Kilcormick were saving turf: however they should not have gathered at all, in a district proclaimed under the Insurrection Act. The yeomanry rode up twice to see what they were up to. Moreover, on the day Murphy rose, Caulfield and Thomas Richards, coming from Dublin, were in Oulart; their purpose to exhort the people to be loyal.

In the case of the rebellion in Connaught, the Anglican bishop Joseph Stock studiously avoided all detail of Catholic priests: however the emphasis by both Gordon and Stock on the idea of stipends from the state for clergymen to relieve them from political pressure from their parishioners suggests that their actual apprehension were substantial.[15] In contrast to Bishop Stock's book, another account by James Little, the rector of Lackan where the French landed, presents a fascinating picture of the modest but real economic gains of the people over the 1790s; and a scenario variously of rising expectations, and of some families going down in the world but hoping to restore their fortunes by radical causes.[16]

Even when the United Irishmen in Dublin finally committed themselves to an all-embracing structure in late 1796, the old divide repeated itself. While the theory of a general structure required units or cells on the ground as the basis of forming a county organisation, the leading United Irishmen in Wexford wanted to create a county leadership structure ahead of or even without strength in depth within the county. Recruited largely through Matthew Dowling in Dublin, they belonged in essence to a prominent and politically ambitious group in the early society of 1791-4. Of these Bagenal Harvey was the most prominent. As comparative moderates they were more concerned with politics than military action, and, as far as military action went, favoured waiting for the French to arrive before rising. Hence they were not pressed by a sense of the urgency of creating small units and of turning them quickly into military cells.

From a divided executive in Dublin, two competing influences radiated outwards; one concerned almost exclusively with county organisation on paper, another concerned with creating a mass cell structure and of arming it. In 1795-6 before a formal structure was finalised, radical groups were already forming in Dublin: they were drawn from United Irishmen and from Defenders alike. Hence, unlike the pattern of north Leinster and north Connaught of incorporating an existing defender cell structure into a spreading United Irishman organisation, there was no uneasy relationship between the two movements as in Ulster and it's borders. Coalescing in Dublin, they recruited for the organisation, though in competition with the more complacent of the two elements in the leadership groups, which was more interested in chiefs than Indians. Significantly the driving force radiated out from Francis Street, was in some respects independent of and preceded the leadership interest, and was helped by missions far afield in the south by three Northerners, Hope, McCabe and Teeling.

In consequence, a political divide existed in the south Leinster counties which was deepened by the approaches adopted by the radical opposition in the general election of 1797. While the withdrawal from politics by the more radical elements of the opposition was followed faithfully in Dublin, Kildare and Down, a divide took place in both Carlow and Wexford, where the election was contested vigorously. The more radical element in county politics around the Grogan interest did not participate. Edward Hay for instance seems to have done so, and his sour comments, whether true or false, on Lord Mountnorris, whose son-in-law was a candidate, are those of a man who had earlier worked closely with him. Cloney, apparently not yet an United Irishman, was also an activist on behalf of Mountnorris in the election.

This cleavage widened the division among United Irishmen in Wexford, where it helps to explain the animosity between Thomas Dixon and Edward Hay, a prominent figure in a group of 'moderates'. This boiled over into the events of Wexford during the three week occupation of the town, and is reflected in the balance of four in his favour and three against, as Hay thought, in the infamous tribunal proposed by him. In Kilcormick, which was precociously organised as early as March 1797, the election may have created tensions. Kilcormick was slow to accede to pressure from the Mountnorris interest (which included Edward Hay) to support the loyalty campaign in April 1798. The divides ran deep. John Hay, an activist of 26 May, and Fitzgerald, an inactive figure of 26 May, had fought a duel at an earlier date. Edward Hay was later silent on his brother (a fact commented on by Miles Byrne), and Hay's account of John Murphy is extremely hostile.

Interests in the eastern baronies of Wexford, notably at Monaseed and Kilcormick, were organised independently of the county interest in 1797 and were supported by visits from the Francis Street emissaries who organised south Leinster. In west Wexford, formal organisation in Scarawalsh and Bantry was at first totally lacking. Kelly became a United Irishman in Dublin, probably through Matthew Dowling, but subsequently abandoned the cause. This absence of organisation may explain why, although Cloney took part in the 1797 election, no tensions lingered on there. There was no existing leadership interest, as there was in east Wexford, and when Kelly and Cloney were recruited or re-recruited, they were in a position to commanded a unified group. They were keen to act, and probably belonged to the group who wanted early action, and ahead of the arrival of the French if necessary.

Likewise the relevance of Kilcormick is in part due to the fact that it was activist, and moved quickly into the field on the opening night. Murphy's own role is in part an accident of the absence of Kyan, Perry and Fitzgerald, but he may have been an officer. The later references to priests stopping bullets or to invulnerability are part of a black propaganda based on documents which were spurious and confessions which smacked of having being forced.

Recruitment for the United Irishmen was made easier by the weakness of government. In January 1798, the two key spies, who the authorities hoped would provide evidence to convict the imprisoned United Irishmen, were tampered with and prisoners, including the most formidable of them all Samuel Neilson, were released. The belief was widespread that the government could not contain the movement. There was a rush to join the organisation; some wanted the titles of captain and colonel. Neilson in his later evidence to the Secret Committee put his finger on things: many saw the organisation as the strongest party in the state. Certainly, the arrest of many of the Leinster executive on 12 March was a serious blow, but in essence it removed the more moderate group (if 'moderate' is the right epithet to describe revolutionaries), and left two competing interests, centred on Neilson and Sheares, in the dominant hardline block which now controlled the executive.[17]

In March 1798 Abercromby, the commander in chief, and the government were at loggerheads in public on security, a fact which seemed to underline the near-total disarray of the Castle. Abercromby wanted the army centralised for action against an invader; others wanted it decentralised to support a more vigorous local security policy. The issue of free-quarters was a charade as even loyalists had no enthusiasm for their widespread deployment on the ground: it was merely the excuse to disperse the army. However, the political struggle was not over till the famous order of 30 March, which introduced what is inaccurately described as martial law.

In fact, as a further illustration of the limitations on government action, the civil courts remained in force: the government had already been seriously embarrassed at the spring assizes in Wicklow and Wexford by the freeing of all the prisoners detained in both counties. Only in April did oppressive methods – selective flogging and house burning – begin in Wicklow, Tipperary and Kildare. Similarly, in Wexford the North Cork militia did not arrive until late April, and oppressive methods began only in the week before 26 May, and the atrocities, though serious, were small in number. The magistrates meeting in Wexford on 23 May involved a tug-of-war between two groups of magistrates and the deferral of a general policy for a further fortnight.

The longstanding divide between the 'moderates', those United Irishmen who wanted to await the arrival of the French, and others explains why Harvey and Edward Fitzgerald of Newpark were so hesitant. The impetus for action came from others in Kilcormick, Monaseed and Bantry and the initial uneven response reflected less the leaders' per-

Death mask of Cornelius Grogan, Johnstown
Castle, Wexford. From the Madden Catalogue.
He was hanged on Wexford Bridge,
28 June 1798.

sonal qualities than their associations in the wider question. The fact that
they may have been partisans of the Sheares brothers, and not of the even
more active Neilson faction who issued the final orders for rebellion may
also have widened the gulf with their associates.

Thus, some of the Wexford leaders seem to have been doubly divided
from the Dublin leadership. First, before 12 March, they seem to have
been part of the 'moderate' interest which favoured a rising after the
French landed rather than one, more recklessly, before they arrived.
Second, they seem in the following weeks to have had their ties with the
Sheares rather than with the Neilson faction. That in turn caused problems for them on the ground in Wexford, as the lower ranks in the cells
of the organisation had been built up even in their own baronies by
activists from Francis Street rather than by the east Wexford leadership.

Of course, in the case of Wexford in 1798 the two central features are,
first, the comparative success of the rebellion, and second, the evidence
of killings which might suggest that the rebellion was purely sectarian. It
is hard to fall back on sectarianism as a general explanation. Firstly, many
Protestants were liberal, and their Yeomanry units were variously inactive or restrained in their behaviour. After the rebellion they remained
friends of the Catholics, and their support was vital to former rebels in
fighting off charges in the courts. The Beauman marriages to Catholics
took place after the rebellion; the Richards ties with the Talbots continued to remain close; a county political interest in support of Catholics
rights was stronger after the rebellion than before, and dominated county
politics for the next two decades.

Secondly, on the Catholic side, sectarian behaviour, though it existed
and is most evident in the curious case of the forced baptisms, was not

universal. We have to be careful about apologias, but the arguments of James Gordon are probably true. He spoke well of Philip Roche, less well of John Murphy. Some Protestants were immune in Wexford, like William Hatton, Mayor Jacob and the Richards; in general this was true of the Quakers was well. James Alexander in several writings made this point also.

A liberal party in the county, allied to the Catholic cause, continued and weakened only in the 1820s. The attempt to restore it in the early 1830s was what prompted Cloney with O'Connellite support to publish in 1832 his account in rebuttal of attempts to stoke once more the fires of sectarianism. The idea that the rebellion of itself had immediately changed everything is false. It is written back from the perspectives of the Protestant conservatism of the 1870s and 1880s, and of the rampant Catholic triumphalism of the same period which was quite happy to emphasise the gulf between Catholics and Protestants.

Dublin in 1798:
The Key to the Planned Insurrection

Thomas Graham

A military dimension was implicit to United Irish organisation even during its legal, constitutional phase (1791-4). The early societies of both Dublin and Belfast had emerged directly from the radical remnants of a paramilitary body, the Volunteers. Within a year of its inception the Dublin society attempted to re-constitute the city's Volunteers as French-style 'National Guards' (with crownless harps as insignia), a project speedily suppressed by government towards the end of 1792.[1]

I

By the following spring Britain was at war with revolutionary France and any manifestation of internal democratic dissent on either island was speedily suppressed. This imposed its own inexorable logic on the situation: with the possibility of constitutional advance blocked, especially as a consequence of the 1793 convention act, revolution seemed as feasible as reform. The recall of Fitzwilliam in the spring of 1795 dashed any lingering hopes of constitutional reform. The consequent escalation and spread of uncoordinated Defender activity convinced United Irish leaders of the necessity for a credible alternative strategy. According to MacNeven, 'from the time we had given up reform as hopeless, and determined to receive the French, we adopted a military organisation'.[2]

From then on the military strategy of the United Irishmen was determined by the French alliance. They were to organise and arm themselves, await the French (who were expected to bring the necessary additional quantities of arms and ammunition), and act as auxiliaries when the time came.[3] The feasibility of this strategy was demonstrated by the near-success of the Bantry Bay expedition in December 1796. Such was the fear on the part of government of the spreading 'secret spirit of insurrection and outrage' (in contrast to the earlier 'open disturbances' of the Defenders so successfully and brutally suppressed by Carhampton in Connaught), that its forces were scattered throughout the country as a police force.[4] If the French had managed to land in large numbers, it

would have taken the best part of a week to assemble an effective force to
engage them, long enough for the French to march all the way to Dublin.
It was a near-success, however, which also induced a degree of complacency into United Irish organisation. Unreliable elements flocked to its
ranks and the initiative began to pass to the government side from the
spring of 1797 onwards. Thus when in June 1797 the Ulster leaders
pressed their Dublin comrades for action there was no credible alternative strategy nor the military capacity (outside of Ulster) to put any into
effect.

The Leinster societies had been requested to adopt military organisation two months before.[5] On 14 May the informer Leonard McNally
claimed that a 'military committee' had been established in Dublin and
two days before Edward Boyle reported that 'out of every tenth man in
every society one is to be chosen who is to act as sergeant and out of that
number they will choose superior officers', i.e. ten sergeants were to elect
a captain and ten captains a colonel.[6] Yet there is no evidence for elections of military officers for this period, certainly not of colonels. Nor
was the Dublin organisation properly armed. According to James
McGuckin, the Ulster movement's chief legal adviser who turned
informer a year later, Dublin had neither arms nor military organisation
in June 1797.[7] This lack of military preparation goes some way to
account for the Dublin leaders' opposition at that time to calls for an
immediate insurrection from the Ulster leaders.

Efforts were made to remedy these deficiencies in the second half of
1797 through the adoption of a new constitution and the expansion of
the organisation in Leinster, which created the conditions for an alternative military strategy, an insurrection based on native resources, with or
without French support. Such a strategy demanded that the initial and
decisive blow be struck at Dublin, the country's capital, hub of its economy and its centre of communications.

The purpose of the new constitution, adopted in August 1797, was to
make the civil organisation more adaptable to the military. Emmet,
O'Connor and MacNeven, in their memoir, referred to it as 'the military
constitution'.[8] The smaller simple society of twelve (reduced from a maximum of thirty-five in the 1795 constitution) was to double up as a platoon commanded by a sergeant. Ten sergeants elected a captain who thus
commanded a company of 120 men, equivalent to the numbers organised
by a lower baronial committee. Every ten captains within a barony or
division (in the case of Dublin city) elected a colonel who thus commanded a regiment or battalion of not more than 1,200 men. Assembled
together, the colonels constituted the military equivalent of the county
committee. They submitted a short-list of three names to the provincial

directory, one of whom was appointed adjutant general, in military command of the entire county (or city, in Dublin's case).[9]

Each of the ranks had their own distinctive insignia, for sergeants a simple green ribbon, for captains a harp with reversed laurel leaves, for colonels a harp with shamrock leaves and for adjutants general a harp unstrung, bearing the motto 'Ireland forever'.[10] Their duties were also clearly defined. Each man was to equip himself with a haversack containing a week's provisions, a kettle or pot, a can and spoon, straps for wrapping up a great coat or blanket, and pieces of green material for putting on pike heads in order to frighten cavalry. Every four sergeants were responsible for a spade, a fork, a pick and a bill hook each. Captains were responsible for one good horse and cart per company, its standard (on a two-foot square piece of green cloth, mounted on a ten-foot pole), and its bugler. Colonels were responsible for the supply of gunpowder and were to ensure that each regiment had its own bullet-mould and someone proficient in using it to make ball cartridges. It was recommended that they, and the adjutants general above them, had either army or militia experience, in order to drill the captains, who in turn would drill the sergeants, who would drill the men.[11]

The adjutants general were the lynch-pin of each county's military organisation. They assessed the quality and quantity of their own forces, those of the enemy, the lie of the land (bridges, fords, roads, etc.), possible sources of provisions and fodder, and were to communicate regularly and directly with the leadership in Dublin.[12]

II

What was the relationship between the civil and military structures? Thomas Reynolds claimed that colonels could attend all meetings within a county but could neither vote nor act as delegate in any capacity.[13] Yet Reynolds himself was both a colonel and one of Kildare's county delegates on the Leinster provincial committee. McGuckin described a similar overlapping of functions at a meeting at Saintfield, County Down in March 1798:

> At first he considered the meeting to be a civil committee, but in the course of his attending at it he found that the members of the committee were colonels in the United army and that the committee met upon civil as well as military business.[14]

But according to Reynolds:

> if they [colonels] were civil officers, the civil department would

necessarily be neglected during their absence, whereas the meetings so low as the baronials are intended to be always continued.
For these reasons you will seldom meet the uppermost gentry at
the committees, as they by being in military employ have access to
all meetings, acquire every information and not being obliged to
attend are less exposed to danger.[15]

Of all the organised counties in Leinster, Dublin was one of the least
prepared in late 1797 and early 1798, when the new structures, military
and civil, began to be put into effect. Military organisation did not begin
in earnest until February 1798, when the Leinster executive appointed a
'Military Committee' to prepare plans of operation for either a French
invasion, or an insurrection without the French if forced into it by government repression.[16] On 25 February McNally, with typical hyperbole,
informed the Castle that United Irish organisation in the city was now
'perfectly military and in its construction ingenious'.[17] The reality, if the
better-placed spy Thomas Boyle is to be believed (20 February), was that
a number of companies, led by officers no higher than captains, were
being formed and trained in the use of firearms and pikes.

At some time in March Boyle reported 'that it was under consideration, that when prepared, *which they were not near being*, whether it
would be right to call all [i.e. United Irishmen from surrounding coun-
ties] into Dublin and attack the Castle or to attack locally'. This was the
strategic dilemma facing Lord Edward Fitzgerald and the delegates of the
military committee from Dublin, Kildare, Meath and Wicklow, who had
been entrusted to draw up a plan of attack.[18] Should the attack on the city
come from within or without? Obviously it would be better to seize the
city from within before government troops, largely concentrated in the
Loughlinstown camp twelve miles to the south-east, had time to reach it.
But how were sufficient rebel troops to be infiltrated into the city without causing alarm?

The solution was to delay the insurrection until the Dublin organisation was strong enough to deliver the internal blow itself, supported by
co-ordinated external attacks from the surrounding counties. This in
turn was to be the signal for a general insurrection in the rest of the
country in order to tie down government troops locally and prevent
reinforcements reaching the capital. If the steadily increasing returns of
men for Dublin were anything to go by, Lord Edward's 'curious state of
paralysis', Pakenham's assessment of his decision to delay the insurrection for another two-and-a-half months, was justified and made sound
strategic sense.[19] In an undated information, probably from the spy,
Edward Boyle, Myles Duignan, a city colonel, told him that 'as soon as

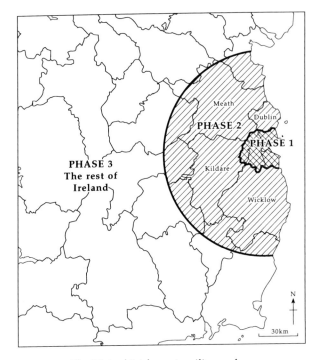

The United Irishmen's military plan

Dublin was ready to rise notice was to be given to six adjoining counties'
within a six mile radius or three hours march of the capital. Half their
forces were to march on the city while the other half-kept government
forces in the country at bay.[20] In the middle of May Samuel Sproule
reported that although the 'violent' lamented the delay because of the
progressive weakening of the organisation overall, it was still gaining in
and around Dublin.[21]

According to Emmet, O'Connor and MacNeven, the military committee did nothing as a committee before the 12 March arrests, but some
of its members on an individual basis drew up instructions for adjutants
general in the event of a French landing. There was no general plan of
insurrection before then, but they admitted that individuals may have
drawn up local ones, for example for the taking of Dublin.[22] This
amounts to a tacit acknowledgement that there was in fact a general plan
or at least one in the making. What constituted a general plan if not the
sum-total of its local parts, and in particular its most important part, the
plan to take the country's capital?

Although Lord Edward Fitzgerald avoided arrest on 12 March, his
papers were seized, and one in particular which outlined the tactics for

urban warfare, a clear indication that detailed preparations were afoot for an insurrection in the city:

> It is supposed that the Enemy have a well appointed and disciplined standing army. In such a Case every Man ought to consider how that Army could be attacked or repelled, and what Advantage their Discipline and Numbers might give them in a populous City acting in concert with the adjoining Counties. It is well known that an Officer of any Skill in his Profession, would be very cautious of bringing the best disciplined Troops into a large City in a State of Insurrection, for the following reasons: His Troops, by the Breath of the Streets, are obliged to have a very narrow Front, and however numerous, only three Men deep can be brought into Action, which in the widest of our Streets cannot be more than sixty Men ... and should they be attacked by an irregular Body armed with pikes or such bold Weapons, if the sixty Men in Front are defeated, the whole Body, however numerous, are unable to assist, and immediately become a small Mob in Uniform, from the Inferiority of Number, in comparison to the People, and easily disposed of ... Perhaps at the same Moment, they may be dreadfully galled from the House-tops, by Showers of Bricks, Coping Stones, etc., which may be at Hand ... as they are regulated by the Word of Command, or Stroke of the Drum, they must be left to their individual Discretion, as such Communications must be drowned in the Noise and Clamour of a popular Tumult ... part of the Populace, who could not get into the Engagement, would be employed in unpinning the Streets, so as to impede the Movements of Horse or Artillery; ... at the same Time the neighbouring Counties might rise in a Mass and dispose of the Troops scattered in their Vicinity, and prevent a Junction or a Passage of any Army intended for the City ... The apparent Strength of the Army, should not intimidate, as closing on it makes its Powder and Ball useless, all its Superiority is in fighting at a Distance, all its Skill ceases and all its Action must be suspended when it once is within reach of the Pike.[23]

Within nine days of the arrests (21 March) the Castle was given details of the plan of attack within the city. The Workhouse division was to attack the Castle; the Barrack division the bank in Mary Street; the Rotunda division the Customs House; and the Green division Trinity College, aided, no doubt, by the fifth column of active student United Irishmen within.[24] Apart from some minor variations, this was to remain the strategic plan of the city rebels and the one they tried to effect on the night of 23 May. On 17 May an anonymous informant, who gave accurate figures for returns of men, stated that the cash in the bank was a particular object.[25] And on 20 May Francis Higgins' spy, a member of the city committee, repeated the objectives of the rebels – in this instance Beresford's bank was preferred to the one in Mary Street, the Castle, the Customs House and a chain of rebels around the city. He gave a detailed description of the plan to take the Castle, the particular responsibility of his own Workhouse division. A large body of men were to pour through Postern Gate from Ship Street. The front entrance was to be seized by Cork or Derry militia. Five hundred others were to descend by short ladders into the Castle Yard from a tailor's shop in Hoey's Court.[26] Information received after the outbreak of rebellion followed the same general pattern.[27]

III

So much for the plans. What actually happened (or did not happen) in Dublin on the night of 23 May? A satisfactory answer is crucial to an understanding of the overall shape of the rebellion. Why was there no apparent rising in the city?

On 11 May Camden informed London that a rising was expected in the city – 'Orders have been given, as some of the lower orders who give us intelligence have informed us, that they should provide pikes and be ready if called upon to rise ... in 13 or 14 days time' (i.e. 23 or 24 May). This had been confirmed to the informer Thomas Reynolds, while on his way to Dublin under arrest, in a message passed to him by a Yeoman sympathetic to the rebel cause.[28] Although the accuracy of this information was to be proven subsequently, the Castle was unconvinced at the time. Its spies were in lower civil committees and therefore not privy to the overall military plan. Their information was, consequently, scrappy and often contradictory in its detail.

The arrest of Lord Edward Fitzgerald on 19 May was a shattering blow to the United Irishmen, but not an entirely fatal one. Preparations for a rising continued, with Neilson at the head. On the day the Sheares were arrested, 21 May, Neilson brought the date for the rising forward by a day, to the night of Wednesday, 23 May.[29] The Castle's best-placed spy, Samuel Sproule, was still not sure if the rising was to be on Wednesday or Thursday.[30]

Wednesday 23 May dawned with the Castle still unclear as to the timing, the place or even the form of the rising. That morning Sproule had been dispatched to the Loughlinstown camp but had little to report – 'their movements are so quick and changes so many that few of themselves know where they will be six hours hence'.[31] Sproule lived in Cork Street and had a number of contacts in lower committees from the area. He was also 'a gentleman of property in the County' and his out-of-town connections furnished him with his best source, an unnamed silk merchant from Lucan, in the barony of Newcastle. The silk mercer was not particularly prominent in the organisation but it so happened that Lucan was the venue for the last-minute co-ordination of the rising. What remained of the Leinster executive met there with a 'deputy from the north' on 15 May and 'deputies of every company in Dublin' also met there.[32] It was a logical venue for the co-ordination of the efforts of Dublin with the surrounding counties, particularly with Kildare, which was expected to provide the core of the intended rebel advance on the capital. The Lucan silk mercer was lieutenant to the local United Irish captain, John McMahon, who also had an address in Phibsborough. From a wealthy Sallins family, McMahon, a failed country grocer, had both naval and artillery experience and later fought alongside Holt in the Wicklow mountains. Although only a captain, he played a pivotal role in the liaison between Dublin and the surrounding counties and was thus privy to crucial military information.[33]

A second report from Spoule reached the Castle at 4.30 p.m. McMahon had left instructions with his lieutenant to mobilise their company in half an hour. Two deputies had been dispatched, one each to Kildare and Wicklow, in order to raise them that night. Up to this point the Castle had been expecting a rising the following day, in Dublin only, and according to the unofficial 'Sheares' plan'. But Sproule was still not sure if Dublin was to rise on the same night or the one following (as the Castle expected), after the Kildare and Wicklow rebels had drawn the military out of the city.[34] By 9 p.m. he was still not sure.[35]

The crucial intelligence was not available because it was not until 9 p.m. that Samuel Neilson assembled fifteen Dublin city and county colonels in Church Lane (Abbey Street, according to Cox), produced a map and assigned each a post to occupy.[36] The main rendezvous points were Smithfield on the northside and Newmarket on the southside. Presumably orders were also given to intercept the mail coaches in order to rouse the rest of the country. There is no further report from Sproule on 23 May extant in the rebellion papers. According to Alexander Worthington, a north County Dublin gentleman and regular purveyor of information, writing to the Castle four years later, the crucial information, of a rising in the city at 10 p.m., was communicated to him by Thomas Boyle at 8 p.m., and thence to the Castle.[37] Since this was before

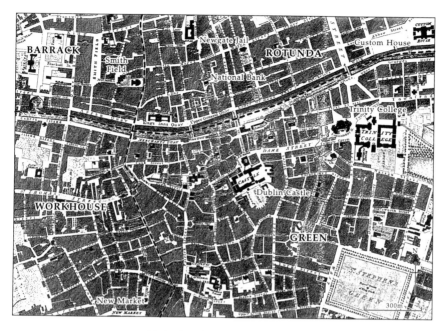

United Irish targets in Dublin

Neilson's meeting with the colonels in Church Lane, we must assume that Boyle knew the time but not the place of the intended rising. It may not have mattered. A glance at a map of the city and the Castle would have deduced that Smithfield and Newmarket were the only places in the proletarian quarters of the city suitable for the assembly of large bodies of men.

According to Barrington, the Yeomanry occupied Smithfield, 'considered as the *probable* point of attack ... as night approached' (about 9 p.m., the very time when Neilson assembled Dublin's colonels).[38] He described the scene with irreverent hilarity:

> The gradations of their discipline and enthusiasm were, however, extremely amusing; those who had imbibed their full quantum of generous fluids, were the most fierce and enthusiastic; others who had dined on substantial matters were as steady as posts. But those who had paraded before dinner, after standing under arms for some hours, could endure it no longer, and a forced loan of cheese, tongues, and bottled porter, from a Mr Murray, of Great George's-street, was unanimously decided upon and immediately carried into execution.

He had an equally jaundiced view of the military tactics involved:

> It [Smithfield] ... formed altogether one of the most disagreeable positions in which an immense body of demi-disciplined men and horses ever were stationed in solid mass, without any other order than, 'if you are attacked, defend yourselves to the last extremity'.

The cavalry and infantry were, in some places, so compactly interwoven, that a dragoon could not wield his sword without cutting down a foot soldier, nor a foot soldier discharge his musket without knocking down a trooper. The cavalry being elevated, could breathe freely in the crowd; but the infantry could scarcely avoid suffocation. A few hundred insurgents, with long pikes, coming on rapidly in the dark, might, without difficulty, have assailed the yeomen at once from five different points.[39]

Barrington's worst fears were never realised. The mere presence of massed ranks of Yeomanry at the rebel rendezvous points was sufficient to persuade the small bands of rebels attempting to assemble to return home. Nevertheless it was a close call. According to Musgrave:

> The rebel drums were to have beaten to arms an hour after ours ... if they had preceded us by ever so small a space of time, the fate of the city and its loyal inhabitants would have been decided; for the mass of the people, armed with pikes and other weapons, were lurking in lanes, alleys and bye-places, ready to start forth on the first beat of their drums, and would have occupied all the streets and assassinated the yeomen before they could have reached their respective stations.[40]

Neilson, meanwhile, left the meeting of colonels and headed towards Newgate jail in order to reconnoitre it for an attack to liberate its prisoners (Lord Edward, Oliver Bond, Henry Jackson, etc.). This action of Neilson has been condemned as quixotic[41] but it is difficult to see why. What Dublin lacked more than anything else on the night of 23 May were leaders of national stature and Newgate was where most of them were held. His decision to reconnoitre the jail personally may seem unwise in retrospect but who else was there to perform the task? He was, after all, effective commander-in-chief, and he may also have been unwilling to delegate the task, in order to avoid admitting to the colonels and lower committees that he and Sweetman were the only members of the executive still at large.

The idea of attacking Newgate and liberating the prisoners was not some last-minute alcohol-induced notion on Neilson's part. A detailed commando style plan of attack, involving 'thirty of the most desperate men' armed with daggers, had been drawn up and Sproule warned the Castle of this on 21 May.[42] Neilson may have abandoned the attempt in the face of John Sheares' threat to reveal all to government if he persisted.[43] Instead, according to Musgrave, a larger scale military operation was decided upon for the night of the rising itself. The Barrack division colonel, Thomas Seagrave, was to have commanded his regiment in the operation. His musketmen were to have kept up a constant fire on the jail from Halpin's distillery in Pettycoat Lane while another party scaled its walls. But it was not to be. Neilson was recognised by Gregg, the jailer, and arrested after a great struggle. According to Musgrave: 'On this fortunate event, some 1,000 rebels, who were to have co-operated with him, and were on the tip-toe of insurrection, having lost their leader, disappeared'.[44]

After this series of disasters it is not surprising that Dublin's rising fell apart before it even started. Not only had the Yeomanry occupied Smithfield, Newmarket and other rendezvous points but they had also barricaded the Liffey bridges, seriously impeding rebel communication within the city, and set up checkpoints on the main approach roads and canal bridges, effectively blocking large-scale rebel infiltration from without.[45]

Given this unfavourable situation what is remarkable is not so much the absence of rebellion in the city but the degree to which the attempt was made at all. According to the Revd William Bennet, former private secretary to Westmorland and later bishop of Cloyne, and therefore well-informed, there was physical evidence to prove it:

> As the rebels came in detached bodies to parade in the places marked out for them, they found them already seized by the King's troops, and after sunrise the lanes and alleys to Smithfield and other posts were found full of pikes and muskets which they had dropped and thrown away in their precipitate retreat.[46]

Meanwhile thousands of rebels attempted to converge on the metropolis from the surrounding county to reinforce their city comrades but were stopped by the Yeomanry barricades or else stopped short themselves once they realised that the rising had not gone according to plan.[47]

The events of the evening of 23 May and the early morning of 24 May were not quite the fiasco described by Pakenham. Bennet presented a fairly sober assessment of the potential threat the rebels represented:

Neilson was one of the most determined and intelligent of all the rebel leaders, and it was entirely owing to his and Lord Edward Fitzgerald being apprehended that the night of the 23rd passed over so quietly. The columns of the rebels which surrounded the town waited one for the other to begin, and had any daring officer been found to lead his men under fire, the others from Ringsend, Eccles St., Clontarf and Harold's Cross in all which places were large bodies of them, would have probably followed the example, which might have been of the worst consequences as the garrison was so weak, and the troops from Loughlinstown Camp did not arrive till two in the morning.[48]

When considered within the framework of an organised, planned, rising, albeit one that had gone wrong, the events in the surrounding county and beyond begin to make more sense. Contrary to Pakenham's claim, that the rebels constituted a 'great mob of peasants', without a coherent military strategy, the United forces did attempt to effect the plan agreed upon.[49] Rebel armies began to mobilise on the night of 23 May in the sur-rounding counties – Wicklow, Kildare, Meath and north County Dublin – and by the morning of 24 May held a crescent of positions within a twenty-five mile radius of the capital, effectively sealing it off from the

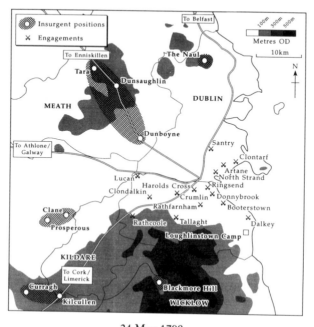

24 May 1798

rest of the country. Their task was to deal with local government forces before advancing on the city.

Three mail coaches had been stopped; the Belfast mail at Santry; the Athlone mail at Lucan; and the Cork mail at Naas.[50] True, not all of them were stopped. The Enniskillen mail coach had managed to dodge the Meath rebels gathering at Dunboyne, while the Cork mail had given Dublin rebels the slip at Clondalkin before it was stopped by a party of Kildare rebels under Michael Reynolds at Naas. If the mail coaches were stopped *after* the rebels of Dublin and the surrounding counties had risen then this could hardly have been the signal for a rising that had already begun! These counties had no need for a mail coach signal to rise. They had been kept directly informed of the overall plan, including the role of the mail coach signal, which was to rouse *the counties beyond*, in Munster, south Leinster and Ulster. Otherwise why would Michael Reynolds have taken the initiative and stopped the mail at Naas unless he knew its purpose? This would also explain the delay before rebellion broke out in the 'outer counties' – King's County, Queen's County and Carlow on 25 May and Wexford on 26 May.

Immediately adjacent to the city, meanwhile, on the night of 23 May, rebel bands from the five surrounding baronies (i.e. within a five to ten-mile radius) advanced into the metropolis, not in order to mount a full-frontal assault from without, but to infiltrate into the city and link up with the rebels within. The unified command structure of Dublin's city and county rebels is evident from the fact that Neilson issued his last-minute instructions to fifteen colonels, too many for the city alone, which had a maximum of eleven. If we take into account one or two absentees, it seems reasonable to assume that the other four or five at the meeting were colonels from the surrounding county baronies.

The intended rendezvous between the county and city rebels never took place, thanks to Boyle's last-minute information, and on the morning of 24 May the rebel bands hovered hesitantly on the edges of the city. Nevertheless Musgrave claimed that 'it was afterwards discovered that many rebels had passed over the bridges before the troops took post on them', although his claim that 3,000 entered the city on the northside through one particular turnpike seems a gross exaggeration.[51] On the night of 23 May and morning of 24 May there were numerous reports of rebel bands, or actual engagements, around the city; to the south at Dalkey, Booterstown, Donnybrook, Ringsend, Harold's Cross, Rath-farnham and Tallaght; to the west at Crumlin, Clondalkin, Rathcoole and Lucan; and to the north at Santry, Artane, North Strand and Clontarf.[52] There were major engagements in the very north of the county in the baronies of Balrothery and Nethercross but here rebel movements tended to gravitate towards the Meath rebels' camp gathering at Tara to the west.[53]

The intended rising was meant to unfold in three phases. In phase one, various key installations in the city (the Castle, Newgate jail, the Bank of Ireland in Mary Street, the Customs House, etc.) were to have been attacked by city rebels, backed up by rebels infiltrated in from the surrounding countryside within five to ten miles. This was to have been closely co-ordinated with phase two – the establishment of a cordon of rebel positions around the capital at a distance of between twenty and twenty-five miles, which, once securely established, were to have advanced on the city once the rising within had commenced. The mail coach signal was to have been the trigger for phase three – a general rising of the country at large, in order to tie down local government forces and prevent reinforcements relieving the besieged capital.

Within the framework of the intended rising the orders given to the various rebel commanders were as adequate as they had to be and were not without a certain strategic ingenuity. In the event phase two was effected with relative success. Phase three was less successful, with partial risings in Westmeath, King's County, Queen's County and Carlow, but in one county at least, Wexford, it was effected with spectacular success.[54] But phase one – the initial rising in Dublin city – was a complete failure. It was the key-stone of the planned insurrection, which, once it failed to materialise, brought the whole edifice crashing down, and gave the rising that appearance of chaos, spontaneity and improvisation which has so confounded historians of it ever since.

The Battle of Oulart Hill:
Context and Strategy

Brian Cleary

The Battle of Oulart Hill, fought on Whitsunday 1798 is now regarded as the most influential victory of the United Irish Revolution. The nation's first Republic was established at Wexford four days later and was governed by a Committee or Directory of four Catholics and four Protestants. Few Irish battles had more profound consequences.

Oulart Hill confounded the conventional wisdom that untrained men could never stand up to the attack of a professional military force.[1] An evaluation of some recently discovered source material, including an 1817 map of the configuration of the forces involved, shows that far from some shapeless rush of outraged peasants upon a rashly led corps of militia, Oulart Hill was the result of a well-laid battle plan, carried through with singular determination by local United Irish leaders.[2]

The decision to attack the United Army was made by Colonel Foote who had overall command of the government forces on the day. His plan was for a pincer movement by both cavalry and infantry. Major Thomas Lombard who led the militia in the attack, did so in a measured way right up to the last decisive moment. The subsequent loyalist accusations that he had acted recklessly is unsupported by the best account of the battle from an actual participant. Local traditions of the battle have naturally thinned with time. That which remains in the oral tradition tends to be very specific to localised occurences and no longer retains an overview. Nevertheless it confirms and amplifies the story in several valuable respects. This account combines the available written and oral sources and places them in relationship to each other.

I

Oulart was an important market village in the eighteenth century. Situated on the old Dublin-Wexford coach route, it boasted one of the few hotels in north Wexford, McAuley's Inn. The owner, Daniel McAuley, had two young sons John and Jim who had joined the United Irishmen.[3] McAuley's Inn was a natural communication point between the Dublin Directory and the local Unitedmen. In the Oulart area the leadership element was provided by the Byrnes of Kilnamanagh and the McAuleys. In Blackwater to the east, Sparks, Etchingham, Murphy and Cullen (Ballyvaldon) were the leading figures; with John Cooke Redmond and his brother Michael in the Castle Ellis area. In the west and north, Murphy, Donovan, Gough and Gahan were in charge in Boolavogue; while Esmond Kyan and Henry Roche headed up the Mount Howard men. To the south in the Ballagh area, Tom Sinnott of Kilbride and Miles and Michael Doran of Mountdaniel (his nephews) were the key personnel.[4] These were all prosperous middle-class families. Indeed Tom Sinnott of Kilbride and his brother Nicholas, who was parish priest of Oulart, were the wealthy descendants of a leading and extended family in the Oulart area prior to the Cromwellian orgy of confiscation. The two Redmonds were descended from the Killagowan family of Catholic gentry. In 1798, Oulart was clearly at the heart of an area that was well organised by those who were the natural leaders of their communities.

On the afternoon of Saturday 26 May, the Dublin coach arrived in Oulart en route to Wexford. Two passengers alighted. First was the Catholic bishop, James Caulfield, loyal to the Government and totally opposed to the advent of French Republicanism in Ireland. He was followed by United Irishman, John Hay; former officer in the French Army; and brother to Edward Hay of Ballinkeele, a pivotal figure on the political wing of the United Irishmen in the county. The place was thronged with people. Some were handing in makeshift arms to the magistrates to procure 'Protections'. Others attended to wait on news from Hay from the United Irish Directory in Dublin.

The bishop, sensing the mood, addressed the crowd warning them of the dangerous course they were taking . He later recalled how:

> On my return from Dublin the day before the rebellion broke out here, I met a great number of men at Oulart, giving up their pikes to three or four magistrates, who administered oaths of allegiance to them. I stopped there about an hour, advising and exhorting the people to peace, good order, and allegiance to his majesty and government, and due obedience to the laws, and denouncing the vengeance of heaven and of the offended laws of the land, which they must bring down on themselves by a contrary conduct.[5]

John Hay, on the other hand, brought a despatch from the Dublin Directory. It is not clear if it ordered Wexford to rise or to wait for the French. Hay walked through the assembled men telling them to go home

McAuley's Inn, Oulart (1890)

and to hold on to their weapons.[6] Within hours small bands of men began to assemble across north Wexford that Saturday evening and Sunday morning.[7] The first recorded raid for arms was at Pipers of Tincurry around six o'clock on Saturday evening.[8] This was the start of the United Irish Revolution in Wexford.

The Dublin Directory's plans for Wexford's Unitedmen were to take over the county and hold it. They were not initially required to leave the county. The national strategy was that the crescent of contiguous counties around Dublin would assist the metropolitans to take and hold the capital. Wexford on the other hand was required to take the county, to isolate Duncannon Fort and to hold its hinterland for a French landing.

Government forces were inadequate to hold the county should a widely supported revolution get off the ground. From the establishment point of view, it was vital that it be quelled instantly. The cavalry was relied on as the force of first response because of its speed and mobility and most of all because of its local knowledge. Should the cavalry fail to prevent the revolutionaries from concentrating in large bodies, then both cavalry and infantry would combine to hold the situation until regular army support could arrive.

On receiving news of the incident at Piper's, Isaac Cornock, the yeomanry commander at Ferns, sent to Camolin for cavalry support to investigate. When they arrived, he split the corps, sending half to Piper's of Tincurry under Lieutenant Smith and the other half under Lieutenant Thomas Bookey to the house of John Boyne, a United Irishman living just beyond the Harrow. It was ten o'clock when Bookey rode out over Milltown Bridge towards The Harrow with his twenty-strong detachment.

Bookey's platoon of cavalry rode into an ambush at the Harrow. All except two of the cavalry turned and fled leaving Bookey and his lieutenant. Immediately after this, Father Murphy sent young Jerry Donovan from Boolavogue to advise the areas from Oulart to Castlebridge that a significant clash had taken place and to confirm a rendezvous arrangement at Darby Kavanagh's of Ballinamonabeg on the morrow. On his way, young Donovan would have spoken with the Oulart leaders Morgan or Peter Byrne who were his uncles.

As he rode by house and hamlet he shouted the news that the fighting had started. William Lacy, an innkeeper some three kilometers south of Oulart, remembered a rider going the way and shouting in the night:

> Get up! Get up and fight! Or you will be burned or butchered in your beds. The country is in a blaze all round you.[9]

Raids for arms became a priority. Loyalist homes had to be raided and where resisted, the houses were burned. With the yeomanry already burning houses where the occupants were absent, there were hundreds of houses on fire before morning. From their own records we know that in the twenty four hours following the Harrow, the Camolin Cavalry burned 'upwards of 170 houses belonging to rebels whose inhabitants had fled' as well as 'the Popish chapel of Boolavogue'.[10]

Father Murphy proceeded to raid Bookey's and other loyalist houses for arms. It was not yet dawn when he led his men east over Dranagh Hill towards Oulart. In the distance the signal fires and houses were burning all around. At Baldennis below Raheenduff he was joined by another group of men from the Monamolin or Buffer's Alley area who came via Clone Cross. From here they crossed over Oulart Hill. Dawn was breaking as they continued down into the village where the Oulartmen were already gathered. On the arrival of the Boolavogue and Buffer's Alley men they were told that at least seven well armed yeomen had resorted to the house of the Revd Robert Burrowes, a field away from the village. It was resolved to commandeer their weaponry. Burrowes was killed by misadventure in the raid on his home. His death was later misrepresented in the post rebellion propaganda in an attempt to portray the United Irishmen activities as part of a popish plot or a pogrom of Protestants.[11]

Some ten guns to the good now, the Unitedmen marched southwards to Castle-Ellis via Ballybrega. There they were joined by a party of about forty men from Blackwater led by George Sparks, a local Protestant landholder. It was now about nine o'clock and the party was some four hundred strong. They moved on to the village of Ballinamonabeg, two kilometers further South. There they met the men of Garrylough, Screen, Ballymurn and Castlebridge under Edward Roche. They now numbered six hundred as the contingents from the different areas combined according to plan.

Meanwhile two hundred men of Hawtrey White's joint cavalry corps had left Gorey in the early hours of Sunday morning. Normally three hundred strong, they were under strength as several men had absented themselves to make arrangements to evacuate their families from the countryside which they had goaded towards insurrection. White's corps burned several houses and shot scores of people almost indiscriminately, some in their own doorways, in the course of his march.[12] He passed through Oulart without delay and came up with the Wexford Army at Ballinamonabeg.

As White approached at about a mile distance, Murphy, Roche, Byrne and Sparks prepared to meet him at Ballinamonabeg. They drew their men up on high ground over the road which ran in a sort of glen at that point. It was an area of small fields and high ditches with good hedges. Sparks showed considerable initiative by running some men behind the ditches on each side of White's approach to outflank the advancing horsemen as deeply as possible.[13] Seeing the enemy drawn up to engage him in countryside very unsuited to cavalry, White withdrew. It was a sensible decision.

White's cavalry withdrew via the Island and Killenagh to Gorey. This marked the first significant morale boost to the Unitedmen now gradually taking on the role of a Wexford Army. They had forced the cavalry to withdraw. However, they did not pursue them. Instead they waited for further recruits and were ordered some time later to march to meet the Kilmuckridge contingent around midday at Ballyscough near The Island en route to Oulart Hill. They were ordered to raid the houses of Henry Bolton of The Island and Darcy Howlin of Ballinahown for arms as they passed. This points to the possibility that both these men may have been involved in the collection of arms at McAuley's Inn on the two previous days.

The United leaders stayed on at Ballinamonabeg where they held a council of war in Kavanagh's public house. The meeting was abruptly terminated when word arrived that units of militia and cavalry were rapidly approaching from the direction of Wexford. In the meantime the expanding Wexford Army had been joined at Ballyscough by its largest contingent, the men from the Macamores and Kilmuckridge. These latter men were akin to the men of Shelmalier barony in that they were used to fowling on the coast and had some fowling pieces. The expanding Wexford Army was now about a thousand strong including many unsworn men who had joined them along the way. Many of these had no arms whatever, having handed them over in the preceding days. From Bolton's they marched via Ballinahown, arriving on Oulart Hill at two o'clock, about the same time as the militia and cavalry were leaving the burning pub in Ballinamonabeg.[14]

On their arrival on Oulart Hill the Wexford Army were met by a large gathering of perhaps a thousand people, including women and youths, who had assembled since morning. With several hundred homes now in flames, they had nowhere else to go. Some of these were now armed with an array of makeshift weapons.

II

The old Gaelic name for Oulart Hill is *An Screig*, meaning stony ground. Although it is only 170 metres above sea level at its highest point, it affords a 360-degree view of almost the entire county of Wexford. It lies like a great whale on the landscape with its steep blunt nose to the north. Its broad back flattens out into a gently curving plateau that is about a hundred metres wide and about a kilometre long. Only on the western and northern sides is the gradient very steep. The southern and eastern slopes are gradual. It is subdivided into many small fields and in 1798 was cultivated to the top.[15]

It is clear from the position chosen by the Wexford Army that their strategy was to exploit the smallness of the fields and fight defensively; to draw the enemy towards them and thus to come to close quarters with them where their chances were best and would compensate in part for the lack of guns. Having to cross the ditches separating the small fields would break up the attacking force at the moment of impact and the ditches themselves would afford cover and comfort for their own men, whether seeking to conceal themselves or to move around the area. Such small fields would also greatly diminish the value of any cavalry that might come against them.

The Wexford Army leaders anticipated the danger of a pincer movement coming against them and moved to counter the threat by taking up a position *below* the summit. This meant that they were never visible to both arms of the pincer movement simultaneously. This precaution was to play an important part in the coming battle.

While they now knew of the force advancing against them from Wexford, they did not know if other units were on their way from Gorey, Ferns, Camolin or Enniscorthy or any combination of them. This was largely neutralised as a problem however, as all the roads from these towns converged towards the south-east of the hill at Lower Oulart. The side of the hill facing these roads was also the gradual slope. For these reasons it was almost inevitable that any attack must come from this direction. Recognising these factors, the fields chosen were on the eastern slope of the hill facing the anticipated attack.

The hill had been reconnoitred in detail by the Unitedmen long before. Now they placed their pikemen in the two fields, designated for the purposes of this article as Byrne's Field and Roche's Field just below it. This main body of pikemen extended from Roche's Field right up through Byrne's Field. It was here, in Byrne's Field, that the people were gathered behind the main body.

Directly below Roche's field was a row of particularly narrow fields running down to the Ferns road that ran across the foot of the hill towards Lower Oulart. A direct advance up these fields was unlikely because of their narrowness, especially when there were much larger fields running up the hill parallel to them just to their south and to the front of the Wexford Army. Local tradition confirms that this was the route taken by the attacking force now approaching.

Anticipating that the attacking force must take this route, an ambush was laid by the Wexford Army that would give them a measure of surprise; maximise the use of their limited firearms, and permit them to come to close quarters without too much loss. Murphy, who had overall command on the day, took personal command of the ambush.[16] It was a large ambush comprising some three hundred men. Centred on the point where the three townlands of Kyle, Oulart and Monawilling meet, it ran in two directions at right angles from that point.[17] One wing ran down eastwards towards the village for about two hundred metres. The second wing ran southwards almost to the site of the monument erected in 1948 to commemorate the tradition which held that Father Murphy stood at this extremity in the early stages of the battle (Map A).

An entrenchment had been dug along this upper wing which was designed to give it cover should it come under attack from the rear by way of pincer movement from the westward by supporting infantry or cavalry (fig. 3). These entrenchments, which are shown on Cahill's map and which are referred to by Cloney, show how the Wexford Army's

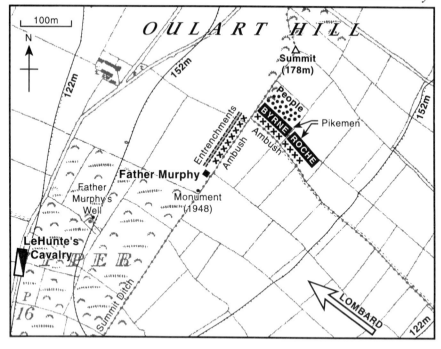

A – Opening phase

position had been carefully planned in advance.[18] Their construction was simple and was probably achieved in the weeks prior to the Rising by the innocent looking work of repairing the ditch: the new and no doubt higher ditch now forming the breastwork, while the gripe from which the clay was taken became the entrenchment. Their guns came to about fifty pieces of variable quality. All firearms were placed at the upper end of the ambush and around the right angle in both directions. Elsewhere, the ambush consisted mainly of men armed with pikes. There were some men of sundry arms and even stones in all sectors of the ambush, hoping that the chance of rushing the enemy would arise.

With Father Murphy in command of the ambush, Edward Roche and Morgan Byrne formed up the remainder of the core Unitedmen. Armed mainly with pikes and an assortment of makeshift weapons they formed up to the rear of the ambush. Edward Roche held the command in the lower and smaller Roche's field, while Morgan Byrne had the command in Byrne's Field. Behind Byrne's body of pikemen, the local people waited anxiously.[19] Byrne was assigned command in this sector because the locals would defer to him as their natural local leader. And so they waited for the hated North Cork militia.[20]

III

Although the 'North Corks' had spent only a month in Wexford prior to the Rising, they left a painful memory of flagrant cruelty and gratuitous torture. Perhaps their most infamous legacy was their introduction of the pitchcap to County Wexford. In the strained circumstances of the time their flaunting of supremacist orange insignia was regarded as particularly provocative. Magistrate Edward Turner of Newfort had been first to bring news of the Rising to Wexford town in the early hours of Sunday morning. His report was soon confirmed by a growing stream of loyalists coming into town with reports that 'the country was up'. The officer in charge for the time being was Colonel Foote. At about eleven o'clock, a detachment of 110 volunteers, from the 150-strong North Cork Militia detachment in the town, was readied to march to Oulart and put down the disturbance. Foote's second-in-command was Major Thomas Lombard of Lombardstown in County Cork, whose forbears had fought under Sarsfield. [21]

The Militia was to be joined en route by nineteen members of the Shelmalier Cavalry under Le Hunte, making a force of 129 in all. Ten of these yeoman cavalry were Protestant, including Turner, and nine were Catholic, including Walter Redmond, great granduncle of John, the future leader of the Irish Parliamentary Party. [22] As Foote led the 110 Militia, who had volunteered for the mission, out from Wexford that morning, they had no conception of defeat. Sallying forth across the new wooden bridge over the Slaney in the direction of Oulart, Foley tells us that their wives and camp followers called after them to 'bring something handsome home!'

Having no guide, the Militia took the more roundabout coast road, only meeting up with the cavalry at Ballyfarnogue. From there they proceeded immediately towards Oulart. When they reached Ballinamonabeg, they burned Kavanagh's pub, but an attempt to burn the chapel was stopped by Armstrong Browne, a Protestant member of the cavalry. [23] It was two o'clock when they marched off for Oulart Hill. Having marched from Ballinamonabeg, Foote halted his force of militia and cavalry on the ridge of Bolabee probably close to the end of the Taypot Lane. Across the valley they could see part of the fledgling Wexford Army drawn up to meet them on the side of Oulart Hill, up near the summit. Foote and his officers considered the situation and planned their attack. Here the story becomes filled with the contradictions employed to save face for the defeat now pending. Foote says that he wanted to retreat to Wexford when he saw the strength of the force opposing him. [24] Yet the combined manoeuvres now embarked upon clearly point to the fact that the decision was made to send the cavalry around to the rear of the hill while the Militia would attack from in front and drive the Wexfordmen into the arms of the cavalry. With this strategy decided, they descended into Lower Oulart, where two roads branched off to the left. The first turned off for Enniscorthy and fifty metres further, on the second road turned off for Ferns. The modern Oulart-Enniscorthy road did not then exist.

As the battle proper now began to take shape, Le Hunte and the cavalry prepared to move off to the left, up the old Enniscorthy road, to cut off the expected retreat of the Wexford Army. Before doing so, Edward Turner, a magistrate and member of the cavalry, set fire to a number of cabins at this turn in the hollow with the intention of luring the men from their strongpoint on the hill. The men on the hill did not respond. With the cabins blazing, the cavalry set off up the road. Gaining the top of the steep rise of ground which brought them almost to the same elevation as Oulart Hill itself, they left the Enniscorthy road, and turned right to come round at the back of the hill, forming a pincer movement. As they came across this height, they halted at the junction with Drover's Lane. Here they burned more cabins, but the men on the hill still waited impassively.

Tension was now very high among the men of the Wexford Army, who did not know the whereabouts of White's cavalry. It was suspected that they might have doubled back from their retreat on Gorey and were now lurking to their rear. As the cabins blazed, a quiet descended on the hill. Peter Foley, who was there, recalls that 'there was no shout of defiance'. They held their position and waited for the impending attack as the cabins burned furiously in the dryness of that hot Summer. Le Hunte continued down to where a bóithrín ran in along behind the hill. At no stage in the battle did the cavalry leave this bóithrín.

While the yeomen were thus engaged, Lombard marched the Militia forward, along the Dublin Road in the direction of Oulart. In full view of those on the hill now, he moved his little force off the road to the left and up what has ever since been called the North Cork Lane. This lane, still extant, headed directly towards the United Irish position but stopped short where it cut the Ferns Road at the foot of the hill. From the lane he had a perfect view of the relative merits of all approach routes up the hill. Reaching the top of the lane, he veered left a few dozen paces and then turned up the hill marching in column through the larger fields.

As Lombard began to climb, things were going well. There had been effective coordination between cavalry and militia in the burning of the houses and in the formation of a pincer movement. The larger fields through which he elected to ascend the hill were considerably more open and they left adequate space between his force and the Wexford Army as a protection against ambush or attack. He could see his enemy sitting on

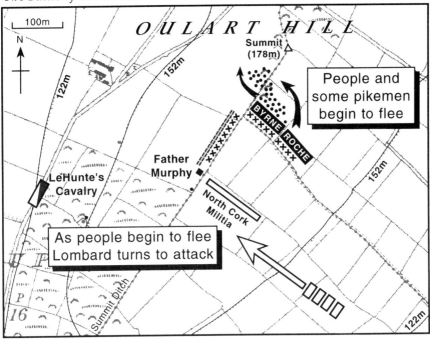

B – Development phase

the hill some four hundred metres ahead of him and two hundred metres to his right. Lombard, preceeded by a drummer, marched his force in column formation, without loss, right up to the same level at which the Wexford Army was stationed.

Lombard proceeded with the planned advance. Ordering a right face he brought his militia to face the Wexford Army. The column formed into a long line of redcoats for the attack. Tension was now at breaking point among the people behind the Wexford Army. As the redcoats formed, 'some of the youths, the timorous and badly armed' in the main body 'began now to retreat'.[25] Lombard could see the expected flight from the Wexford ranks begin (Map B). The conventional wisdom about untrained men was proving correct. Thus to complete the plan by driving the fleeing people before him into the path of the cavalry waiting on the north-western side of the hill, he ordered his line to advance.

IV

Watching Lombard come up the hill from the Ferns road, Father Murphy had stood at the southern extremity of that part of the ambush that ran along the summit ditch. He was needed there to reassure these men who were farthest from the main body and to maul Lombard should he attempt to march out on to the summit to make sight with the cavalry. Now as Murphy and his men watched intently, Lombard faced right towards the main body and began to move across the hill in line formation. Leaving command to a subaltern, Murphy hurried off towards the other wing of the ambush now facing the oncoming militia. There was not a moment to lose. Moving swiftly on foot and fearful of the impact on the men of so many of their comrades slipping away, he encouraged the men with great effect, warning them to hold their positions or face the consequences from the cavalry who he said would be waiting for them:

> They will wait to see us dispersed by the foot troops so that they can fall on us and cut us to pieces. Remain firm, together! We will surely defeat the infantry and then we'll have nothing to fear from the cavalry.[26]

Lombard came on steadily as the tumult and confusion spread in Byrne's Field. John Murphy, now with the ambush, eyed his approach across the intervening ditch. This brought the militia into the adjoining field and heading towards the ambush, which apparently they had not seen. Some hundred and twenty metres from them, Lombard's line began to fire irregularly to accelerate the rout. Peter Foley says no one was hit at this stage:

> As the royal troops advanced to within about twenty perches of us they commenced firing as they advanced but not in regular volleys. The balls whistled by us and over us. We the gunsmen resolved to stand together and not to fire until our enemy would be quite close to us and then to fire and rush in amongst them.[27]

The redcoats approached steadily, marching in line with Lombard mounted on their right. Lombard had every right to assume the cavalry must now create havoc among the fleeing people and that such intervention must destabilise the entire Wexford Army, now in mortal danger.

Unknown to Lombard, the cavalry were halted on the road below. When the fleeing people came over the brow of the hill and saw them, they immediately realised the danger of 'retreating into an open and level country [where they would] be exposed to immediate and certain destruction'.[28] The people paused, but still the cavalry hesitated. This provided a critical respite for Morgan Byrne, to rally the men and prevent panic in the main body (Map C). His dramatic action saved the day

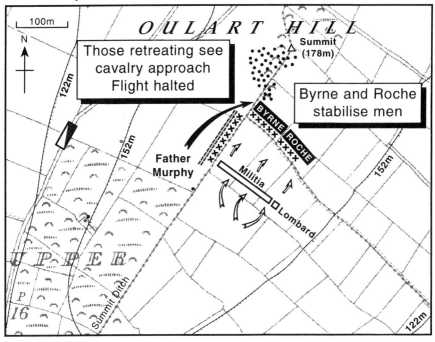

C – Critical phase

for the revolution. Holding aloft the red coat of a cavalryman, he rode through the crowd shouting aloud:

> Shame! Shame! Are you afraid of me because I wear this? No! You are not! It is not the man that you are afraid of. It is the red rag that frightens you. If you met them there below in a fair man for man, would their caps and red coats frighten you ? Not at all. You would soon decide it with them.[29]

With Byrne seizing their attention, the situation steadied. A measure of the danger, and of Byrne's achievement in overcoming it, is the fact that less than half of the main body remained in position behind the ambush, when the battle, now converging was finally joined.[30] Murphy, Roche, Byrne and Sparks now conferred.[31] Sensing that the battle could now slip from Lombard's control, a momentous decision was made. They elected to take the initiative. With the ambush intact, with the cavalry disengaged, and with Lombard advancing, they saw that there was still a chance of victory, despite the loss of half the main body.

  With only half their men remaining, it was imperative to give the ambush full effect in one initial massive blow. To draw the North Corks right in over the ambush, they now pulled back what was left of the main

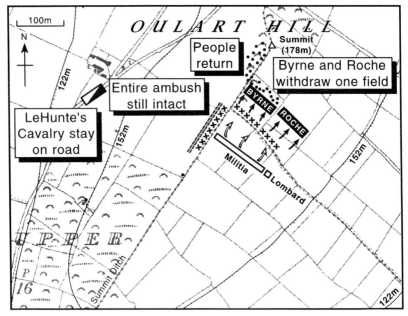

D – Control phase

body of pikemen over the ditch behind them into the next field (Map D). The difficulty was to make it convincing and to achieve this, the Wexford Army leaders kept their heads and left the ruse until the final critical moment available. Peter Foley tells us how this was seen from his end of the ambush in Byrne's Field:

> our little band of gunsmen were on the right of our main body. The ditch at our rear was about eight or ten perches from us. The enemy advanced with a daring boldness up in front of us. Our pikemen – I should have rather said our men of sundry weapons – the greater part of them had now retired behind the ditch just alluded to and even joined by a few of our fugitives who returned on seeing White's division of Cavalry.[32]

The ambush was still intact on the forward ditch, crouched low in readiness for the impact and undetected. As they closed, the North Corks' thin red line extended down the hill and tended to outflank the visible body of pikemen now withdrawn into Sparks' Field. Lombard rode on the right of his line, opposite this critical point. Seeing the main body retire over the fence, and convinced that it was a desperate effort to withdraw the remaining pikemen from destruction, he raised his sword aloft and ordered the charge. 'Up lads!' he cried, 'The coast is clear!' With that

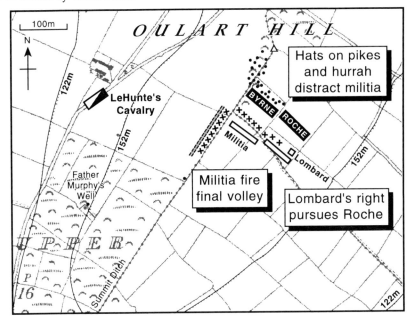

E – Commitment phase

the right of the line rushed to cross the forward ditch.

All was movement now as the forces closed. With the right of the line dashing to cross the ambush ditch in pursuit of the main body of apparently retreating pikemen, Thomas Lombard was irrevocably committed. He no longer had control of his line as a whole. It is not known where Foote was at this moment. When the Militia crossed the ditch on the right, they suddenly saw the ambush to their left. Just then the main body of pikemen in their new position in Sparks' Field, desperate to distract the remainder of the Militia line from becoming aware of the discovery of the ambush, raised their hats on their pikes and gave a deceiving hurrah! (Map E)

In the heat of the moment, the main part of the Militia line fired a volley. Unknown to them, they were at that moment a mere twenty metres from the ambush which now arose before them and fired a volley with sundry arms into their line just in front of them.[33] Fifty weapons firing at such close range must have taken out a third of their force with fatality or injury. The impact was devastating. Immediately, the ambush went onto the offensive. Even as they did so, now that the trap was sprung, the men from the main body were already running helter-skelter along behind the ditches towards the battlefield to outflank the Militia. Peter Foley who was in the ambush takes up the story:

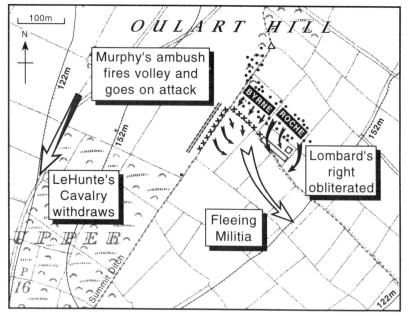

F – Closing phase

A man from … the Macamores stood beside me. He had a stone in
each hand … A man with a brass barrelled blunderbuss was on the
other side … They were now not more than fifteen yards from us.
The man armed with the stones fired one of his bullets and instantly sent the other after it. The first told with such effect on the arm
of one of our assailants that it caused him to drop his musket. I
can't tell if his second round told for on that instant the man on my
other side fired his blunderbuss and I my musket. And 'pop', 'pop'
went a shot from every gun. The conflict had now become general.
Few of us attempted to reload. We dashed in amongst them and in
a summary way we used both breech and barrel of our guns. And
our sundry armed reserve was 'up and at them'.

At close quarters now the advantage shifted to the Unitedmen. The
shock of the ambush and the escalating counterattack on all sides left no
chance of recovery to the Militia. The Unitedmen from the ambush were
in amongst them even as the main body hurtled towards them across the
ditches and threatened to encircle them behind every fence (Map F).
Lombard was one of the first to fall; Tom Donovan of Boolavogue was
the first United Irish casualty. For a few minutes, it was every man for
himself. Then the Militia broke and ran. Peter Foley again:

the soldiers running down the hill firing over their shoulders, the insurgents in amongst them knocking them down with their various weapons, numbers of them with stones of which the hill offered a plentiful supply.

Those retreating spilled down the hill as fast as they could. Some went through the North Cork Lane where they were ambushed a second time by a contingent of United Irishmen from Ballyvaldon who were just arriving in Oulart as the battle got under way. Prominent amongst their leaders was twenty-one-year-old Thomas Cullen of Ballyvaldon who fell the following day in the Battle of Enniscorthy.

Seeing the Militia break and run as they themselves entered the lane on their way to the hill, the Ballyvaldon men took up position behind the ditches on both sides of the lane. Several Militiamen were killed here as they attempted to come through. Sixteen men turned to the right when they hit the Ferns road and dashed by the direct route towards Lower Oulart to get back towards Bolabee. As they rushed down to the village a straggler in their number was killed by a woman with a blow from a kitchen implement. Trying to make Bolabee, the rest made it across the old Wexford-Dublin road at a place called 'The Alley' in the old village, not far from where the cabins were still smouldering at the turn of the steep Enniscorthy road. But the pikemen coming up to them killed ten in Monachan's Bog, where they were buried. Five still raced on for Bolabee. As they breasted the top of the incline near Sinnott's farmyard, three more were summarily despatched. The last two continued on. More than a kilometer further on they were overhauled by two stalwart pursuers Thomas Cullen and Joseph Reilly. In a moment, they were killed. Cullen and Reilly went on to Gaby's Crosses where they found a drunken drummer of the North Corks whom they also killed. The Battle of Oulart Hill was over.

V

Six of the Wexford Army had fallen. Peter Foley tells us that they were Tom Donovan of Boolavogue, Humphrey Crowley of Kilpierce, John Dempsey of Monawilling, a man named Somers from Finchogue and a weaver from Courtclogh whom name has been lost. These five were shot by the Militia. Foley says the sixth man, was a Murphy from Kilcotty, who was killed in error by his comrades because he wore a red waistcoat. He had the bad luck to fall on his face in the action and was piked on the ground by mistake as a redcoat. Father Murphy received a graze on the neck and bathed it in a well on the hill after the battle.

The Militia lost one hundred and five officers and men of their total compliment of one hundred and ten. Colonel Foote arrived back in Wexford with one sergeant and three privates. Foote's nephew, Lieutenant Ware, died in the battle. He was mounted and on the point of making good his escape when a drummer boy called to him. He turned to pick him up but was pulled from the saddle by the hook of a pike.[34]

The United Irish army must have found it difficult to believe their own achievement. They had scored an incredible success. As they moved out of Oulart that evening via Boolavogue and Ballytreacy to camp Carraig Rua, they could not have known that the course of Irish history would change as a result of Oulart Hill. The effect of the battle on morale was felt county-wide. Men now flocked or were ordered to the green standard as loyalists flocked to the towns for safety.

The victory of Oulart Hill roused the people of County Wexford to their assertion in arms of Ireland's sovereign right to democracy. The nation's first Republic was set up four days later at Wexford. Governed by four Catholics and four Protestants in the non-sectarian fashion of the Unitedmen, the Wexford Republic fought twenty-one battles, but fell at Vinegar Hill. There were as many battles fought after Vinegar Hill as there were before, but by then the Republic was no more.

By ushering in the Wexford Republic and the military achievements of the Wexford Army, which at peak numbered 20,000 men including contingents from Wicklow, Oulart Hill assumes its real historic importance. The fact that Irish militiamen died speaking Irish while fighting in the English interest against their fellow countrymen is a salutary reminder of the complex political, cultural and social effects of imperialism. It was from this pernicious system that the United Irishmen, both Catholic and Protestant, fought to extricate their country.

San áit álainn seo, beidh cuimhne ar a n-íobairtí, idir bhua agus bhriseadh, ag sliocht a sleachta go foirceann ama'.

The Military Planning of the 1798 Rebellion in Wexford

Daniel Gahan

For generations scholars have portrayed the Wexford rebels of 1798 as a disorganised force, with little training for battle and without a military plan. Loyalist historians, echoed by Pakenham in our time, have been intent on presenting the rebels as a frenzied mob, inspired by religious hatred and bent on the destruction of Protestants.[1] This school, typified by Musgrave, regarded the rebels as 'savages' and interpreted their warfare similarly, as passionate, cruel and certainly unplanned. Apologists, in the aftermath of the Rising, and numerous nationalist commentators since, have attempted to present the rebellion as a reaction to government severity, rather than a co-ordinated attempt at revolution. This trend began with Thomas Cloney and Edward Hay and reached its cul-

'United Irishmen upon Duty'; a Gillray cartoon;
courtesy of Nicholas Robinson

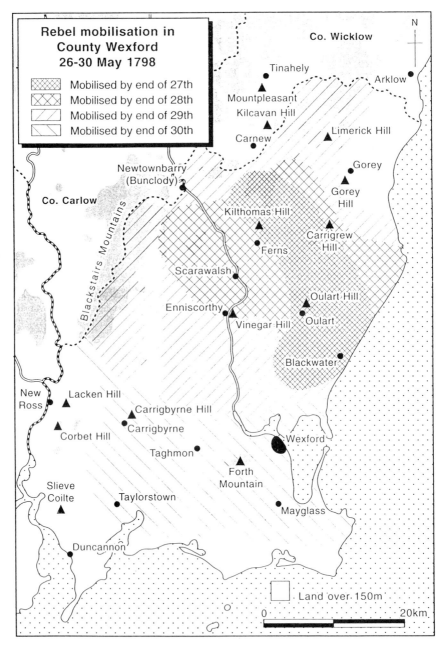

Rebel mobilisation in
County Wexford
26-30 May 1798

Mobilised by end of 27th
Mobilised by end of 28th
Mobilised by end of 29th
Mobilised by end of 30th

Co. Wicklow

N

Tinahely

Arklow

Mountpleasant
Kilcavan Hill

Carnew

Limerick Hill

Newtownbarry
(Bunclody)

Gorey

Gorey
Hill

Co. Carlow

Kilthomas Hill

Carrigrew
Hill

Ferns

Blackstairs Mountains

Scarawalsh

Oulart Hill

Enniscorthy

Oulart

Vinegar Hill

Blackwater

New
Ross

Lacken Hill

Carrigbyrne Hill

Corbet Hill

Carrigbyrne

Taghmon

Wexford

Forth
Mountain

Slieve
Coilte

Taylorstown

Mayglass

Duncannon

Land over 150m

0   20km

mination in the work of Father Patrick Kavanagh.[2] Here too, the Wexford rebel is portrayed as an unwilling fighter, with little training, whose fierce bravery compensated for the absence of larger plan.

Recent work however, has begun to turn this view on its head. Louis Cullen has demonstrated convincingly that the Wexford United Irishmen were well organised on the eve of the rebellion. With the possible exception of parts of the far south of the county; rebels were numerous and were part of a well-coordinated national movement.[3] Nancy Curtin's more recent work on the United Irishmen in Ulster and Dublin reveals the impressive strength and complex organisational character of the movement. Moreover, Thomas Graham's work on the planning of the Rising, outlined above, unravels the details of the United Irish grand strategy which they came to implementing.[4]

According to Graham, the rebellion was initially conceived as a coup than a prolonged revolutionary war. It was to be centred on Dublin, where co-ordinated units were to seize key public buildings and officials and then move out to take control of the entire city. This was to happen in a matter of hours. In the meantime, the counties immediately surrounding the capital (northern Dublin, Meath, Kildare and Wicklow) were to play a vital role of neutralising government garrisons in their own localities, and preventing crucial reinforcements moving towards the capital. Once the city was secured, the local units would move on the city to consolidate the position of the provisional government. Counties immediately outside this inner tier, such as Wexford, Carlow, Kilkenny, Queen's and King's, together with east Ulster, were to play a less direct role in the coup. Their task was to neutralise government forces within their boundaries; they were not expected to march on the capital nor did they expect to operate outside their own borders.[5]

Wexford was among the later counties to develop a strong United Irish organisation.[6] Nevertheless, since it was growing there it may be presumed that United Irish agents discussed military strategy with the more important of the Wexford recruits, especially with those like Esmonde Kyan, William Barker and John Hay who had military experience.[7] Just how far these discussions went and to what extent their content was communicated to the rank and file is uncertain. Yet, it is likely that by May 1798 the Wexford colonels had given consideration to how they would tie government forces and seize control of the county. In Wexford, as elsewhere in the country, the United Irish leadership expected to assemble the parish units, each containing thirty men, at the appropriate time in several central points. These initial mobilisations were to take place under cover of darkness; the rebel battalions were to be ready by dawn to take on the government forces that would inevitably move out from the towns to disperse them.[8]

All over the country, the government campaign of arrests, disarmament and terror which began in late April 1798 disrupted the United Irish leadership. Wexford was no exception. Contemporary accounts indicate that cartloads of prisoners, many of them active United Irishmen, were drawn from the northern and south-western parishes of Wexford in the latter part of May.[9] While the officer ranks of the Wexford movement remained unscathed until 23 May, a day or two earlier, the authorities in Arklow arrested several suspects who linked Anthony Perry of Inch to the conspiracy.[10] As a prominent Protestant from the Wexford/Wicklow border-land and as a rebel colonel, Perry was a critical figure, linking liberal Protestant and Catholic elements in an area riven with sectarian tensions and connecting the United Irishmen of southern Wicklow with those of northern and central Wexford.

Perry was arrested and while he was released after three or four days he remained under careful observation. By the time of his release on 26 May Perry had broken under torture and implicated several United Irish officers in the conspiracy, most notably Bagenal Harvey, Edward Fitzgerald and John Henry Colclough, all from the south-eastern part of the county.[11] Perry did not pinpoint rebel officers in other parts of northern and central Wexford but it appears that at least one other prominent leader from the North, Esmonde Kyan of Mount Howard, was under arrest by 26 May.[12]

Not surprisingly then, the Wexford rebellion which erupted on the night of 26-27 May was effective only in a small part of the county. There was no movement whatsoever in the parishes around Gorey, while rebels in places like Monaseed remained confused about what to do, even though they realised the moment of truth had already arrived. Such confusion is reflected in the fact that Miles Byrne and his companions spent the night making their way southwards from Carlow, where they had gone in a vain attempt to link up with rebel forces there.[13] In addition to this, the movement had been severely disrupted in the south-east by the arrests of Kyan, Fitzgerald, Harvey and Colclough. It appears that word of the Midlands rising had not yet reached the western and south-western parishes, but if it did, rebels there were anxious to await news of a response from their north before making any move.[14] Since that response did not initially come, the hesitancy of someone like Thomas Cloney, even as late as 28 May, is understandable.[15]

Nevertheless, there were signs of planning and co-ordination in the limited area of Wexford in which the rebels did move on 26 May. The outlines of two epicentres, rather than one as has often been assumed, are evident from the information we have of that critical night. The rebels made their move both to the west and to the east of the river Bann around sunset, which on that evening was at about eight o'clock.[16] They conducted hasty attacks on the homes of known loyalists, yeomen or other houses where they suspected arms were being stored. Then, in the early house of the morning, they moved towards larger points of rendezvous.[17] As part of this larger movement, units in the Kilrush/Ferns/Camolin area, marched towards Kilthomas Hill, the highest point in their locality. In addition, rebels from areas between Boolavogue and Castlebridge made their way in the direction of Oulart, the highest point in west Wexford.[18]

The second phase of the uprising was the counterattack by government forces on these rebel assemblies which came early that morning. While the rebels had anticipated this assault it is not surprising that, given the handicaps from which they suffered, the government forces came close to victory. With ease, they drove the rebel army from Kilthomas and, but for the sighting of soldiers off to their north, the rebels on Oulart Hill would probably have suffered a similar fate at the hands of troops coming from their south. Instead, they rallied and annihilated the column of soldiers sent to destroy them.[19]

The rebellion entered its third phase on 28 May. By that point the commanders at Kilthomas Hill had reassembled a remnant of their force

Gathering in May 1938 on the site of the United Irish camp at the Three Rocks; photograph by Nicholas Kelly

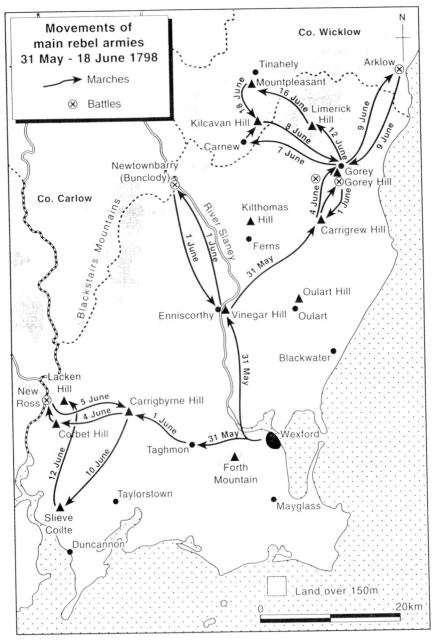

Movements of
main rebel armies
31 May - 18 June 1798

→ Marches

⊗ Battles

Co. Wicklow

Tinahely

Arklow ⊗

Mountpleasant

18 June

16 June

Limerick
Hill

Kilcavan Hill

8 June

12 June

9 June

9 June

Carnew

7 June

Newtownbarry
(Bunclody) ⊗

River Slaney

Gorey
⊗ Gorey Hill

Co. Carlow

1 June

1 June

1 June

Kilthomas
▲ Hill

4 June

1 June

Carrigrew Hill

Blackstairs Mountains

Ferns

31 May

Oulart Hill
▲

Enniscorthy

Vinegar Hill

Oulart

31 May

Blackwater

Lacken
New ▲ Hill
Ross ⊗

5 June

Carrigbyrne Hill

4 June

1 June

Corbet Hill

31 May

Wexford

12 June

10 June

Taghmon

Forth
Mountain

Taylorstown

Mayglass

Slieve
Coilte

Duncannon

Land over 150m

0   20km

N

at Ballyorril, near Scarawalsh, where even before the survivors from Kilthomas arrived, rebels from some of the parishes south of the Slaney had begun to gather.[20] Conscious that their task was to neutralise government forces in the county and given that they had taken control of a crescent-like swath of territory running from Blackwater around to Kilrush, the rebels might have been satisfied to hold onto this gain. They could have done this by marshalling sizable, well-armed forces on the highest points in this area. Were things to work out according to plan elsewhere in Leinster, this might conceivably have delivered the entire county to the anticipated provisional government in Dublin. However, the seizure of at least one strategic town in the county, particularly a central one like Enniscorthy, would guarantee supremacy.

The entire rebel force concentrated for an assault on Enniscorthy. Having captured the town they were joined by units from western parishes, giving them possession of the central third of the county.[21] Significantly, they had turned their backs on Gorey and the surrounding parishes where sectarian hatred was rife; if religious motives had been their inspiration this would have been their first target. Additionally, only a rebel army that assumed that the counties to their north were falling into the hands of comrades could have afforded to face south in this way.

Once taken, Enniscorthy presented the rebels with something of a dilemma. The town had been captured with considerable loss of life and the garrison, small though it was, escaped. At this point the rebel leadership, still without several key figures, was joined by Anthony Perry and officers from south Wicklow; their arrival brought the first hints that things had not gone quite so smoothly in Wicklow and Carlow. As was the norm amongst United Irish officers, the leaders seem to have worked as a committee. They hesitated and argued among themselves as to which direction to take next: towards Wexford Town, towards New Ross or towards Gorey.[22]

On one level, such debate reinforces the impression that the rebel army had no plan and had simply rebelled out of fear for their lives. In the light of Graham's work, however, hesitation at this point is perfectly understandable. They had not driven their enemy into the southern third of the county. They believed the government forces holding out around Gorey had been cut off from Dublin by the Wicklow insurgents and were unlikely to affect to the fate of the capital. There surely was plenty of reason to consider simply holding the ground they had now won; if their task was to tie down enemy forces then they had clearly done so by this time.

Nevertheless the Wexford rebels pressed on. The next day, they

moved to Wexford town and laid siege to the place from Forth
Mountain. This seems to have happened largely because their imprisoned
comrades, Fitzgerald and Colclough, arrived to plead on behalf of the
garrison for them to disperse. The mission amounted to a bait; whether
intended or not it worked. The rebels, against the better judgement of
some of their leaders, were enticed to break camp and march southwards.[23]

In the brief siege of Wexford town which ensued the rebel army continued to exhibit an extreme caution which exasperated men like John
Hay and Miles Byrne.[24] But given that the cost of an assault on the town
would be enormously high and that the war surely appeared to have
been won at this stage, their hesitation is understandable, even if it provided the garrison the chance to escape.

By 31 May, with the county seat in their hands, the Wexford insurgents had driven their enemies from every part of the county, save toe
holds at Gorey, Bunclody, New Ross and Duncannon. Had this been a
solitary, desperate uprising it would have been logical, at this stage, to
consolidate the rebel forces into one huge army. Then this force of
twenty thousand men could swing out into east Munster or the midlands
and attack the capital. Later, historians would argue that New Ross stood
in the way of such a strategy, but a number of facts contradict this assessment of the town's strategic importance on 31 May. It was still lightly
garrisoned; the rebel force could easily have by-passed it and left small
forces to lay siege to the town. Meanwhile they could have spread the
rebellion out beyond the Barrow, into Carlow, Kildare and Kilkenny
with the main body of their forces.[25]

The strategy adopted by the rebels following a contentious meeting
on 31 May was very different.[26] They divided their forces into three
columns, each of which would drive towards one of the government toe-
holds. Once these positions were seized they were to await word from
their counterparts in other parts of the country.[27] Significantly, the
column moving against New Ross, began in a very leisurely fashion; by
that evening they had reached no further than Taghmon. This delay is
explained, in part, by their commander's decision, Bagenal Harvey, to
entertain a large number of people in his town-house, including some
former government supporters. We can only surmise that he was prepar-
ing for the transition to the New Regime by nurturing support for himself on all sides of the political spectrum and, of course, that he was
already assuming the war was as good as over.[28]

Such optimism was misplaced. Everything changed on 1 June; after
that the rebellion in Wexford became a very different kind of struggle.
From this point on, the rebels were aware that something had gone badly

wrong with the rising at its epicentre, the midlands and Dublin. The possibility that they were all alone loomed larger with each day. That day, the rebels suffered unexpected reverses in their efforts to capture Newtownbarry and Gorey. Both setbacks occurred because the arrival of government reinforcements, from points to the north and west of the respective towns, turned the tide in favour of the defenders. This was the first real evidence of trouble which was confirmed with the capture of Lord Kingsborough, the commander of the hated North Cork militia, off Wexford Harbour on 2 June. Kingsborough had left Dublin a day or two earlier and almost certainly told the rebel leaders in Wexford Town of their comrades failure in the capital. Since he had travelled by land as far as Arklow, he would have acquainted them with the strong position the government still enjoyed in County Wicklow too.[29]

From this point, the rebel leaders tried hard to accommodate themselves to the new situation. For at least two days, they delayed their original plan to seize government outposts around the perimeter of the county.[30] Then, between 4 and 9 June, they made desperate attempts to capture such places, achieving modest success at Carnew but failing to take Arklow, and faring disastrously at New Ross.[31] Significantly, at both Arklow and New Ross, there seems to have been serious dissension in their ranks so that Father John Murphy's took no part in the battle of Arklow and John Henry Colclough's men and perhaps several other units failed to attack the enemy at New Ross.[32]

Divided counsel continued to beset them in the days after those battles. There were some sharp disagreements between the northern division, which confined its operations to the Wicklow borderland, and the leadership in Wexford town under Edward Roche and Bagenal Harvey.[33] The northerners wanted to pursue an aggressive approach but the leadership in the county seat preferred to hold their ground. There is even evidence that Matthew Keugh, Edward Roche, Bagenal Harvey, John Henry Colclough and others wanted to pursue negotiations with the government at this stage.[34]

When General Lake finally began his move against the county on 19 June the commanders in Wexford town sought to consolidate their forces within the county and to make a last stand at Vinegar Hill (in which incidentally Roche himself did not participate). Elements of the northern army, based at Kilcarvan Hill, just inside Wicklow, were unconvinced of the wisdom of this strategy. They realised that the time for a conventional war had long passed and expected little in the way of mercy from Lake. Garret Byrne of Ballymanus was particularly prominent in this respect. For at least a week prior to this, he had advocated the adoption of a guerrilla strategy. He had suggested that a remnant of the rebel forces should move into the Wicklow mountains and hold out there until the French landed. This was rejected in favour of Roche's more conventional approach. On the night of 19-20 June, despite the fact that they had Lake's main column checkmated at Carnew, the northern rebel army agreed to withdraw and conducted a frantic forced march southwards in preparation for a field battle in the centre of the county.[35]

The loss of the Battle of Vinegar Hill, partly explained by the absence of Edward Roche and vital units from further south when the fighting began, put an end to the conventional phase of the struggle.[36] Now the stark choice which faced the more prominent United Irishmen in the county was to throw themselves on the mercy of the government, or to adopt Garret Byrne's guerrilla strategy. It is significant that when the two sizeable rebel columns escaped from Moore's and Lake's clutches in Wexford town late on 21 June, they had still not made their minds up as to which approach to pursue.

That night, as they camped at Peppard's Castle, half-way up the county's east coast, and at Sleedagh Demesne, a few miles to the south of Forth Mountain, their leaders debated their options. At Sleedagh, Father John Murphy persuaded the entire rank and file of two thousand men, or more, to follow him into the Midlands in an attempt to link up with die-hard elements he expected to be holding out in parts of Kilkenny and Kildare. What he intended to do after that is unclear but it seems likely that he hoped to rekindle the Midlands rebellion and strike at the capital itself. This was a remarkable turnabout from a man once so dedicated to the 'Wexford only' approach that he refused to take part in the battle of Arklow. Father Philip Roche did not agree, however, and left for Wexford town at dawn the next day, under the mistaken assumption that he could bargain for his life with the victors.[37] In the meantime, the entire rebel officer corps at Peppard's Castle, with the exception of John Hay, agreed to push northwards towards the Wicklow Mountains. The rank and file were less convinced in this case and during the night hundreds slipped away to their homes. The column which left for the northern border of the county the following morning was reduced to a couple of thousand men.[38]

The rebels now found themselves in a situation they had not anticipated; a reality reflected in behaviour and continued indecision. Many of them had probably begun the struggle in the expectation that by the last week of June the first steps towards a constitutional convention would be underway; men like Harvey, Roche and Colclough may even have secretly hoped that they would be involved. Instead, the most important figures in the South Wexford United Irish movement went to the gallows that week, including Harvey, Colclough, Grogan, Keugh, Philip Roche

Major-General Sir John Moore

and Kelly.[39] In the Midlands, in the meantime, Murphy's column failed to revive the rebellion. To make matters worse, the rebel column that had camped first at Peppard's Castle passed the week on the border with Wicklow, waiting in vain for stragglers to join them.[40]

The next logical phase in the struggle should have been banditry, with the fastness of Wicklow as the theatre of operations. Even in the dying days of June and in early July, the old struggle between the desire to take the guerrilla route and to remain conventional continued, however. Thus, we find Miles Byrne and his Monaseed comrades making an heroic trek from Scullogue Gap, in the Blackstairs, to the foot of Croghan, on the Wicklow border, while many other members of the column that had gone into Kilkenny and Queen's county, chose to abandon the struggle rather than resort to the banditry option.[41]

Similarly, once the remnants of the rebel armies had been united at Croghan on 5 July, most of their leaders still favoured the option of marching across tremendously dangerous country to link up with Presbyterian rebels in Ulster.[42] It is indicative of the true nature of the Wexford rebel movement, that it did not end in the kind of mountain banditry that one would expect of a peasant revolt, the kind of 'savage rebellion' that Musgrave suggests it is, or the 'goaded revolt' of the Kavanagh/Dickson model. Instead, the campaign ended in a field at Ballyboghill, County Dublin, with the rebels still attempting to face their enemies with a disciplined line of battle.[43]

   The evidence points heavily, then, in the case of Wexford at least, to the newer explanation for the rising. From start to finish, the strategic options that the rebels chose and the battle tactics they adopted, are consistent with a movement inspired not by those on the margins of this society but by those at its centre. The United Irishmen, everywhere in Ireland and in places like Wexford in particular, were desperate to seize power quickly and to make the transition from the Old to the New Regime smoothly. When this did not happen, they were at a loss and the response of the Wexford leaders to their military problems suggests that most of them, especially those from the southern half of the county, were not the stuff of guerrillas and would never fight as such. This, in the end, may have been their undoing.

Local or Cosmopolitan?: The Strategic Importance of Wexford in 1798

Nicholas Furlong

The insurrection of 1798 in the south-east of Ireland has been compared to the Vietnam War. In each case, one phrase accurately describes the exchanges; pitiless ferocity. I will try to identify the basic reason for that ferocity, not merely in 1798 but in the Cromwellian and Williamite wars of the previous century.

I

In or around 1500, the great powers of Atlantic Europe became acutely aware of the presence of America, a vast continent of immeasurable riches and immense potential. The four major sea powers in question were Portugal, Spain, France and England. To the last three, Spain, France and England, one European country became immediately the focus of urgent attention. That was the island of Ireland, about which the Romans never bothered but the master sailors the Vikings did.

Ireland assumed a critical importance to the expanding naval powers and empire builders, because it possessed geographical qualities, greatly coveted in the perilous days of slow trans-Atlantic sail. Ireland's strategic importance rested on two features:

1. Allowing for the curvature of the earth and the route of the Gulf Stream, the shipping lanes from North America and the Caribbean frequently came along Ireland's west and south coasts. Ireland was the first, or the last landfall on that route for the determined adventurers bearing the flags of Spain, France or England (see Map 1).

2. The Atlantic coasts of Ireland possessed deep harbours which offered long established port facilities and storm protection in addition to the provisions which could be derived from their rich hinterland. Possession of these facilities on the Atlantic's rim was of decisive significance to all three naval powers. The greatest, deepest and safest harbours, noted by all three powers, were the Shannon Estuary, Bantry Bay, Cork which was the most comprehensive of all, Youghal, and lastly Waterford Harbour.

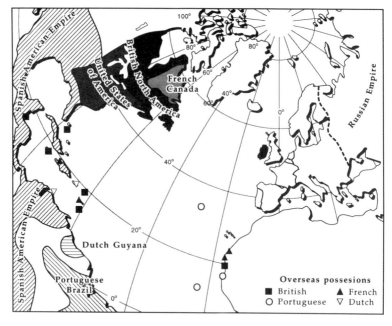

Map 1

An unambiguous example of England's need of these facilities is reflected in Charles Vallency's report to London in 1797. Recalling the
presence of the American privateer John Paul Jones and French men o'
war off Ireland's southern coast during the American War of Independence, the General remarked; 'Cork Harbour, of so much importance to
this island and to Britain, remained in a most defenceless state ... when
the combined fleets of our enemies prevented the regulated convoys of
provisions for America and the West Indies being sent out'.[1] If those pro-
vision ships had not finally escaped the report insists, 'the troops in
America and the West Indies must have been starved'.

Throughout the fifteenth century, the English had little power in
Ireland outside the old Viking enclave of Dublin. In the 1500s however,
this changed dramatically as Ireland became the focus of unprecedented
activity. We find recorded feverish English input in this land as the Tudor
governments implemented a policy of plantation, beginning in Laois and
Offaly (1556). In Queen Elizabeth's reign (1558-1603) this scheme was
expanded to include sites of vital importance to the Atlantic strategies
(see Map 2).

In this period too, we find an emerging Spanish reaction and presence, especially in Waterford and Wexford,which lasted for almost a
century.[2] Wexford's Bullring with its bull baiting sport was a Spanish

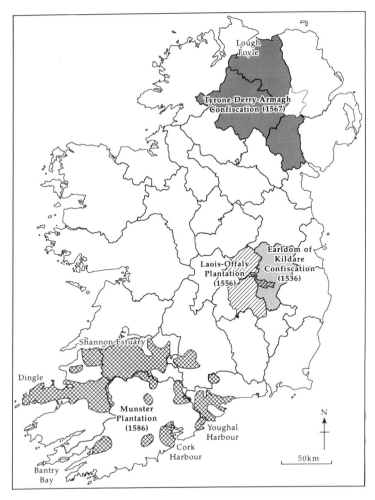

Map 2

introduction. I remember how old Wexford women like Mrs O'Brien of Redmond Road and Mrs Moran of Common Quay would call the southern side of the Bullring (by the Bank) 'The Piazz', the name put on it by the Spanish sailors and which was in popular use down to this age.

These links between Wexford/Waterford and Spain, England's mortal enemy, were maintained and developed through to the 1640s and the 'Great Rebellion' of the Confederation of Kilkenny. Influential contacts were maintained with the Papal Court at Rome and the Royal Court of Spain by the Franciscan Order and powerful Wexford families like the Rossiters and Waddings. A Wexford town rhyme to torment the London personnel went, 'God bless the King of Spain, if it wasn't for him we would all be slain.' During the 1640s, the colours of the King of Spain were hung from the windows of the town and carried through the streets and into the market stalls.[3]

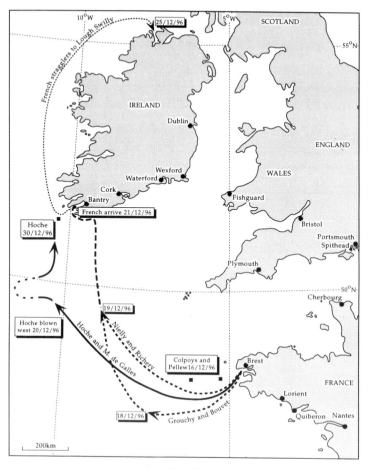

Map 3

Nevertheless, Wexford betrayed its own potential, as frigates operating from the port inflicted havoc on English merchant shipping and men-of-war in the Irish Sea from Holyhead right around to the Solent. Known as 'Dunkirkers', these three-masted frigates, were 170 tons and carried 16 guns along with a crew of 80 sailors and 35 soldiers.[4] It is no coincidence then, that after Cromwell landed in 1649 above Dublin he turned down along the coast to capture Wexford, which he described as being 'famous for being infamous'. There, he put to the sword all he could, hanged the Franciscans and evicted all whom he identified as England's enemies.[5] Waterford held out for a further two years but the zone's peril to England had been highlighted and was eliminated for that century by Cromwell.

General Vallency

II

France was the greatest threat and rival to England's Atlantic expansion in the 18th century. The interminable catalogue of wars between the two need not detain us, but the the American War of Independence and the French Revolution highlighted Ireland's vital geographical position once more. To military and naval operational planners government systems may change sensationally, but the strategic principles remain constant especially since England and France were at war since the Spring of 1793. In Christmas week of 1796, in response to Wolfe Tone's representations, a large French fleet under General Lazare Hoche arrived unmolested into Bantry Bay (see Map 3).

The landing was prevented by the most savage winter storms of that century, but the presence of a French army of 14,500 men and 41,644 stand of arms cast the Irish establishment into chaos. The alarm and terror induced by that narrow escape can scarcely be described, not only in London but amongst the aristocracy, landlords, loyalists and the Churches in Ireland. From what they knew of the progress of the French Revolution and its elimination of aristocrats, clerical and lay, king and queen, their response bordered on the hysterical.

In response to this crisis, in 1797 King George III instructed General Charles Vallency to prepare a survey and a report on the defences of southern Ireland. Vallency produced a thorough examination of the military and naval situation with recommendations. The actual assessment of each port, harbour and landing beach is given from Galway, south and then east to Wexford. Vallency highlighted the significance of Galway, where he predicted the French would take control of the country between Galway and Limerick. He reports that the French would then 'be within two days march of the rebellious class of the north'. The August 1798 French landings in Connaught were not haphazard whatever else.

Vallency's in depth survey of our theatre of war in the south east is of special interest. It can be assumed that the French were as well informed, perhaps better, since we know Napoleon had possession of the extraordinary intelligence that the guns of Duncannon Fort defending Waterford Harbour were defective, a factor of which the English authorities were not aware.[6] Vallency, however, reported that were the enemy to gain the high ground behind the fort the fort was lost anyhow.

Vallency provided King George with a comprehensive description of Waterford Harbour, its tides, its extent as an inlet into southern Ireland, and the possibility of utilisation of its three rivers by the French. 'It is spacious and safe and capable of large ships and where they cannot venture can be reached by transports, light frigates and corvettes which may run up to Passage. Vessels that don't draw more than ten feet of water may run up to Waterford City and New Ross'.[7] The tide rate, he observed, was strong and without a breeze it could carry transports up to the mouth of the Barrow at three miles per hour.

'Opposite Duncannon Fort,' he declares, 'the harbour is more than a mile broad at high water and boats may pass unmolested. A landing in the harbour would be with the design to fall on Waterford.' The report highlighted the facility with which the enemy, the French, could land troops on the many fine beaches, like Woodtown and Dunmore. Vallency concluded that Duncannon Fort was on the wrong side of the harbour for the protection of Waterford City and that the opposite side to Duncannon was defenceless.

Why the emphasis on Waterford City? Quite simply, in the event of a long war or indeed overwintering of a French expeditionary force, Waterford City could billet 6,000 infantry and stable 1,500 cavalry horses with accommodation for its troopers.[8] The French Army, from previous experience and intelligence, knew every square inch of land and river as far even as Clonmel 24 miles from Waterford, and also up the Barrow toward Carlow. Surprisingly however, little attention has been devoted to Waterford's position in the many discussions on 1798. Nor has adequate consideration been given to the French landing, planned for the spring of 1798, which would have involved the collusion of the well focused and connected United Irish leadership in County Wexford.

Then there was New Ross! Again, Vallency notes its potential for provisioning an army. He reports that it sends annually four or five ships of 400 tons to Newfoundland. The enemy he states will find many good places for debarkation on the New Ross side of the harbour as at Loftus Hall, Fethard, Baginbun and could take strong positions with the Slaney on his right and the Barrow on his left. 'He might', Vallency continues 'be then in possession of Carlow in two days, only 40 miles from Dublin and thus turn all the English troops collected at Ardfinnan, Fermoy and Cork'. This, he adds, was the plan of the duc D'Aguillon in the war with England previous to the revolution.

Vallency estimated that New Ross, where the first bridge over the Barrow was situated, was capable of billeting 5,000 infantry men plus 500 cavalry horses and troopers. The General went on to declare that there was no obstacle in 1797 to the landing of between 12,000 and 15,000 men on the western side of Waterford Harbour. On the Wexford side he reported again, for the second time, the practical ease with which the French could land in moderate weather. His concluding overall assessment, put simply and without clinical military and naval details, was as follows: 'if the enemy lands on the eastern shore of Waterford harbour and pushes his advanced parts to Ross or Enniscorthy, he certainly is provided with provisions and the means to penetrate to the metropolis as fast as possible'.

General Lazare Roche, leader of the ill-fated expedition

Wexford Quay

III

I don't think that there is any doubt but that the United Irish leadership in County Wexford was well informed throughout 1796, 1797 and 1798. That was particularly true of the Harvey/Colclough/Boxwell axis on the Atlantic Coast near Kilmore where the direct smuggling of French wines was a long-established art form.[9] Nevertheless, a couple of points remain significant in the early days of the insurrection. Firstly, after the capture of Enniscorthy a conference took place on Vinegar Hill on Monday 28 May which was attended by Father John Murphy and the United Irish chiefs; the south county United Irish leadership was not present, they had been arrested on the previous day. One Enniscorthy man present, William Barker, had a distinguished military record in mainland Europe, where he served as an officer in Walshe's Regiment of the Irish Brigade in the French army. Barker insisted on an immediate march to take New Ross.[10] His eminently sensible advice was not taken. He was outvoted. Wexford was chosen as the next objective.

The second matter of significance was the decision taken after the large and acrimonious meeting of the United Chiefs on the Windmill Hills following the capture of Wexford Town. That meeting took place on the morning of 31 May 1798.[11] After Bagenal Harvey was elected Commander in Chief, a decision was taken which indicated absolute confidence, or complacency, or, in hindsight, excessive optimism. The United Irish Army divided into three divisions, with three separate

Mrs Mary Furlong Hore of
Templescoby, a photograph taken
in 1869 by Vandyke Studios, Liverpool.
She was the sister of Matthew Furlong
and Michael Furlong of Templescoby,
lived through the entire period of 1798
and died in old age.

objectives. It is not without significance that the division headed to take
and pass through New Ross was commanded by the Commander in
Chief Bagenal Harvey at whose side there were the Atlantic Coast
United chiefs, Boxwell, Colclough, Hughes and Grogan, plus the men
under the formidable United Officers John Kelly, Thomas Cloney, Philip
Roche and the Furlongs of Templescoby. For the reason I have indicated,
along with the expected arrival of the French, the Waterford Harbour
zone was the vital immediate objective.

The stakes involved in 1798 were enormous and of world significance.
One of the outcomes was the destruction of England and its society
along with the shattering of its Atlantic power followed, there was no
doubt in their minds, by a fully extended punitive vendetta accompanying their expulsion from their lands and property confiscated in Ireland.

Be that as it may, there is one other over riding factor. It is a factor
which has been buried by propaganda with sorry consequences. That
factor is this: it did not matter in the slightest whether Ireland was inhab-
ited by five million low Church Protestants, Roman Catholics, Moslems,
Jews or Hindus. What mattered most was who controlled the richly
endowed coasts and hinterland of an Ireland placed tantalisingly on the
most important sea route in the western hemisphere.

Miles Byrne: United Irishman, Irish Exile and *Beau Sabreur*

Thomas Bartlett

In his introduction to the 1907 edition of Miles Byrne's autobiography, Stephen Gwynn confessed that 'I owe my acquaintance with these *Memoirs* to Mr John Dillon [the nationalist M.P.] who spoke of them as the best of all books dealing with Ireland: and a reading of the volumes left me inclined to agree with him'.[1] Dillon's assessment, and Gwynn's endorsement of it, reflected the admiration in which Miles Bryne was held in nationalist circles at the time: but later students of the period have concurred in the volumes' worth. Byrne's three-volume history of his life and times, published posthumously by his wife, Fanny,[2] in Paris in 1863 has been variously reprinted since then, culminating in a facsimile edition in 1972.[3]

Byrne's account of his activities in the 1798 rebellion and after holds enormous interest: he possessed a very good memory (though not an infallible one), a lively writing style, by turns dispassionate and sober then indignant and *engagé*, and he was never reluctant to pass judgement on those with whom he came in contact, on or off the battlefield.[4] Crucially, he had fought in the key battles – at Oulart (or Oulard, as Byrne consistently spells it), Enniscorthy, Arklow and Vinegar Hill – and, following the collapse of the Wexford rising, he had taken part in the 'little war' in the Wicklow mountains in the company of Joseph Holt and Michael Dwyer.[5] Later still, he had been heavily involved in Robert Emmet's abortive conspiracy. In short, Byrne's detailed testimony is that of a veteran insurgent (though he had just turned eighteen when the rising broke out) writing with the immediacy of an eye-witness, and is exceptionally valuable for that. Byrne, moreover, wrote as a self-conscious Irish exile: he never returned to Ireland after 1803, and each volume of his *Memoirs* was sub-titled, *Notes of an Irish Exile of 1798*, and can be read as a contribution to the literature of exile.

His lengthy residence in Paris offered him that necessary distance from which to reflect dispassionately on his formative experiences in Ireland but, inevitably and understandably, we find longing and sadness, pride and self-pity jostling each other in his narrative. In some respects Miles Byrne for all his continental travels never left Monaseed, County

Wexford. Revealingly, his first sight of Napoleon Bonaparte in 1803 triggered a Wexford memory: this glimpse of the Emperor, he wrote, 'brought to my recollection the happy days when we used to read at the chapel the newspapers giving an account of his brilliant campaigns from 1795 down to the peace of Campo Formio, October 1797. After the insurrection of '98, he added sadly, 'I could not attend those chapels.'[6]

Finally, Byrne, uniquely among the exiles of 1798, offered what appeared to be an authoritative military perspective on the rebellion in the south-east for his account of the rebellion of 1798 was refracted through his later experience of some thirty-five years' service as an officer in the French army on the continent. It is these perspectives – as youthful insurgent, as Irish exile and, especially as military veteran – that together render Miles Byrne's *Memoirs* of unique value and, I think, help explain its attraction for John Dillon and Stephen Gwynn, and indeed for later readers.

II

On the failure of Robert Emmet's plans, Byrne took ship for France where, in 1803, he enlisted in Napoleon's Irish Legion.[7] After a few years' boring garrison duty in France awaiting (in vain) the order to invade Ireland, the regiment moved to the Low Countries where it was involved in the dismal and inconclusive Walcheren campaign. Soon after, Byrne found himself in Spain (1808-12) where he participated in the storms of Astorga and Ciudad Rodrigo, set-piece battles such as Fuentes de Onoro and, particularly relevant, in the counter-insurgency campaigns against Spanish guerillas. He later fought in Bonaparte's last battles, notably Leipzig but also Lützen, Bautzen and Katzbach (1813-14).

Robert Emmet, leader of the Rising of 1803

In view of his military career under Napoleon – and some not very deft footwork at the time of the '100 days' of Bonaparte's restoration – Miles Byrne was very fortunate to remain in the French army as a half-pay captain (and indeed to stay on in France) after the Bourbon restoration. In 1828, he returned to active service in the French expeditionary force sent to the Morea peninsula to aid the Greeks in their independence struggle against their Turkish masters (1828-30). His conduct on this campaign having been commended, he was promoted *Chef de Bataillon* (or Colonel) in the 56th Regiment and after some years in various garrisons in France, including a period on counter-insurgency duty in Brittany, he retired from the French army in 1835.[8]

Byrne wrote his *Memoirs* in his retirement and he reviewed events in Wexford and Wicklow in part from the standpoint of an active insurgent *and* veteran soldier. Admittedly, other professional soldiers – mostly British, but some French too – have described their campaigns in Ireland in 1798 but they rarely characterised their Irish opponents, or their Irish allies, as anything more than a rabble or a mob.[9] Again, while other United Irishmen and insurgent leaders later wrote accounts of their actions in the 1790s, these memoirs lack either the perspective that a distinquished military career gave to Byrne's account or they are flawed by an understandable anxiety to exonerate the author from the excesses of the 1798 rebellion or to minimise (and sometimes magnify) his involvement.[10]

T.W. Tone's autobiographical writings provide perhaps the most useful military statement of United Irish plans; but Tone contrived to miss the rebellion and never saw action.[11] Similarly the later works of such United Irish 'exiles' as William James MacNeven, Charles Hamilton Teeling and Archibald Hamilton Rowan, while of considerable interest for the 'pre-Rebellion' (the period 1795-8) and the 'post-rebellion' (1799-1803) have little that is first hand to say about the actual fighting in the summer of 1798.[12] On the other hand, 'General' Thomas Cloney of Wexford and William Farrell of Carlow did see plenty of action in 1798 and both penned accounts of what they saw and did, but neither had any previous or subsequent military experience against which to assess the campaigns in which they fought.[13] Perhaps only William Aylmer – first a rebel leader in County Kildare, then subsequently an officer in the Austrian service until the end of the Napoleonic wars and finally, a comrade in arms of the South American liberator, Simon Bolivar – could have revealed an authoritative military perspective similar to Byrne's in his account of the '98 rebellion: but, so far as is known, Aylmer did not commit his adventures to paper.[14]

As an experienced soldier, how did Miles Byrne later view the con-

Sadler's (1869) representation of the battle of Ballyellis

duct of the 1798 rebellion? As the reader will discover, he certainly did not mince his words when delivering his strictures on the leaders of the rebellion, and he was scathing about, as he saw it, their profoundly misguided strategy. He particularly condemned the decision not to advance on New Ross directly after the battle of Enniscorthy. If New Ross had been promptly attacked it would have fallen, he argued, and thus have opened up the inland counties of Carlow and Kilkenny to the insurgents. Instead of this, the rebels opted to capture the strategically useless town of Wexford and thus inadvertently helped contain the rebellion within the county. In addition, they compounded their mistake by establishing a camp on Vinegar Hill, an exposed and, without artillery, an indefensible 'stronghold'. 'How could our generals for an instant think' exclaimed Byrne 'that Vinegar Hill was a military position susceptible of defence for any time without provisions, military stores or great guns!'[15]

Moreover, despite his comment that 'we had a host of leaders who displayed talents of the first order', for the most part, Miles Byrne was critical of the quality of rebel military leadership.[16] Admittedly, he conceded that Beauchamp Bagenal Harvey was 'liberal and patriotic' and that it was useful to have a Protestant leader if only to give the lie to the report that the rising was a 'popish plot'; but equally he claimed that Bagenal Harvey 'did not possess the military talents or qualities necessary for such an important rank and situation'.[17] And he lamented that two of the rebels who had seen service earlier in the Irish Brigades of the French Army – William Barker and John Hay – had little influence in the conduct of the campaign.[18] Indeed, Byrne complained bitterly that the defects in the chain of command on the rebel side were such that 'we were often at a loss to know from whom the orders came'. Again, he alleged that the inability on the battlefield to distinguish at a glance rebel officers from the 'rank and file' was productive of further confusion; and he expressed his anger that 'our generals', in the event of a reversal, 'did not seem to have any preconcerted plan of action'.[19]

Byrne placed great weight on the supply difficulties of the rebels: 'It was a depot of military stores which we wanted most' he noted.[20] Provisions were always a problem on account of the looting and devastation wreaked by both insurgents and crown forces, and so too was an adequate supply of serviceable muskets and sutiable ammunition. Some 20,000 rebels, claimed Byrne, marched on Arklow but between them they could hardly muster 'two thousand firelocks fit for use' and these were frequently of different calibres and it was impossible to get cartridges to fit them.[21] 'It was our total want of ammunition even for the arms we possessed, that caused our failure', noted Byrne in his account of the battle of Vinegar Hill.[22]

Not that Byrne was an enthusiast for the musket: far from it, for he realised that in the hands of an untrained person it would accomplish little. According to Byrne, because most of the muskets in use in the rebel army had been seized by 'country people little accustomed to use them, the locks soon became deranged', and he went on to bemoan the fact that 'many of our men, as soon as they got any kind of firelock, even an old pistol which could not fire a shot, gave away their pikes to others'.[23] Naturally, in view of the havoc wreaked at the Battles of Oulart and Ballyellis, he was full of admiration for the offensive qualities of the humble pike, 'this powerful weapon', when employed amongst the hedgerows of County Wexford.[24]

Finally, Byrne was dismissive of the way that General Humbert had conducted his campaign in Ireland in September 1798. Simple vanity, alleged Byrne, prompted Humbert to seek open battle with the 'English army' whereas his proper course of action had lain in taking to the mountains, awaiting reinforcements and soliciting support from the Irish soldiers in the opposing army.[25] In general, Byrne was convinced that the rebels should have practised 'avoiding general battles and of all things not seeking to defend weak positions like Vinegar Hill', for if this were done then 'we should be able always to outmarch the English infantry and defeat them in detail'.[26]

It should not be inferred from Byrne's weighty criticisms of the rebels' conduct that he found little to praise in it. On the contrary, Byrne was filled with pride as he described the deeds and heroism of the likes of Anthony Perry, Edmund Kyan, Fr John Murphy and Thomas Cloney. 'I had been in many combats and battles' previous to the engagement at Vinegar Hill, he wrote, 'but I never before witnessed such a display of bravery and intrepidity all along our line for nearly two hours until our ammunition was expended.'[27] It was, however, those who displayed military talent whom he most respected. He called to mind Mathew Doyle before Arklow: 'I could not help admiring the clever military manner he kept his men manoeuvring, marching and counter-marching in the presence of the enemy ... He was at the head of about two hundred fine fellows, all keeping their ranks as if they had been trained soldiers, and strictly executing his commands.'[28] Perhaps a little wishful thinking entered into his recollections of his own Monaseed corps in the retreat after Vinegar Hill? He claimed to recall 'our division marching in perfect order' into Wicklow, executing a manouevre 'with great skill', and maintaining 'formidable close order'.[29]

III

As noted above, Miles Byrne had barely celebrated his eighteenth birthday when he embarked on his career as an insurgent, and his comments on the campaigns in which he fought were, in part, his response to some of the books which had since been published on the rebellion. Byrne was angered at Edward Hay's attempt to minimise the level of United Irish organisation in Wexford and, equally, by Hay's determination to play down the role of the Catholic priests in the rebellion.[30] He was scathing about those 'would-be patriotic writers on Irish affairs' who drew a veil over atrocities by Crown forces in 1798 and he was dismayed by R.R. Madden's open hostility to Robert Emmet in his study of the United Irishmen.[31] Especially, Byrne waxed indignant at the claim – mostly by Protestant writers – that the rebellion in Wexford had been entirely a religious uprising, a peasant fury, with massacre and plunder as its guiding objects.[32] In his pages, it is rather the crown forces who have murder on their minds; it is they who roam the countryside burning, torturing and shooting innocent civilians.

Byrne was not blind to the atrocities committed by the rebels – for example, at Scullabogue and Wexford Bridge – but he was adamant that they formed no part of rebel policy. On the other hand, he contended that greater outrages by crown forces – the burning alive of the rebel wounded in their makeshift hospital, for example – enjoyed the hearty approval of the authorities. Time and time again he stressed the discipline of the rebels, whom he called the 'Irish army', against the ruffianly behaviour of most of the 'English army'; the Irish Yeomanry he dismissed as 'only good for shooting the poor defenceless people in cold blood'.[33] In his discussion of his campaigns in Spain, he noted that his low opinion of English soldiers was confirmed by their sack of Badajoz (1812), in contrast to the scrupulous French behaviour at other storms. For his part, he was not at all surprised at the English army's behaviour 'from the knowledge I have had of the cruelties committed by the regiment of Ancient Britons in my own unfortunate country, Ireland, in 1798.'[34]

Byrne was surely being disingenuous here. The 'English' army which sacked Badajoz included many Irish soldiers, notably the Connaught Rangers: and while the Ancient Britons did indeed have an unsavoury reputation (for which they paid dearly at Ballyellis), no serious writer has ever contended (Goya saw to that) that the French counter-insurgency policies in Spain were anything other than draconian. At best, it might be argued that it would be difficult to determine on which side – Spanish or French – the balance of cruelty lay in the guerilla war in Spain, but no one could seriously suggest that the French were blameless.[35]

It is revealing that the counter-insurgency aspect of Miles Byrne's service in Spain is dealt with in a cursory fashion. It might have been expected that a former Irish rebel would have noted points of contrast and comparison between the rebellion in Ireland and in Spain. But Byrne devotes only a few paragraphs to his activities in putting down the Spanish *partidas*, or guerilla bands:

> The guerillas at this time (1809) though far from being organised as they were afterwards gave great occupation to the French troops in the province of old Castille. It became a very disagreeable service to be continually night and day marching to disperse those bands and quite repugnant to our feelings and we wished much to be brought to fight against a regular army.[36]

On one occasion, he mentions his discovery of the bodies of eighteen French soldiers slain while on escort duty, but he passes on quickly to other matters, and there is no mention of French reprisals.[37] In fact, Byrne was well aware that he could be criticised for acting in Spain as the English acted in Ireland. His answer to that charge was contained in his detailed account of an animated discussion between himself and a

Miles Byrne at the age
of 42, drawn by his wife

Spanish priest concerning the morality of French intervention in Spain.

While serving in the Asturias, Miles Byrne was billeted overnight with the parish priest of a village. On learning that he was Irish, the priest remarked to Byrne that he had studied at Salamanca, that he had known many Irish during his time there, and that he had met some Irishmen who were now serving in the Spanish army. Did Captain Byrne not consider 'that there was a great similitude in many respects between the people of our respective countries, their sufferings etc?' Captain Byrne did not. 'There could be no comparison' he retorted, 'as in his [the priest's] country at that moment the inhabitants were not persecuted and deprived of their civil rights on account of the religion they professed'. Moreover he traced the treacherous history of Spain towards the French Republic and the Empire since the early 1790s and contended that it was understandable that 'a sure guarantee [of non-aggression] was required by the French government from the Spanish'.

The Spanish priest's reply went straight to the heart of the matter: 'The war is carried on against you', he stated, 'because we want Ferdinand [the lawful Spanish King] more than Joseph [Bonaparte's brother, and the usurper] ... because we want to remain a Spanish nation independent of foreigners and we hope it will never cease till the last French soldier is driven from our country. You are here in a province, the Asturias, which the Moors could not conquer and', he added, 'with God's help you will fail also'. Byrne professed to admire the 'patriotism of this enthusiastic ecclesiastic' but, rather than return to the argument, he preferred instead to muse at length on 'the virtuous clergymen who suffered torture and death as martyrs both in the field and on the scaffold, in Ireland, in 1798', and he went on to discuss the life and death of the two Fathers Murphy, and Fathers Roche, Redmond and Kearns.[38]

Miles Byrne's evasiveness concerning his role in the guerilla war in

Spain was no doubt prompted in part by his sensitivity to criticism like that voiced by the Spanish parish priest. However, too much should not be made of this: in the end, Miles Byrne was a soldier in the French army and would undertake whatever duties – however 'disagreeable' – were assigned him, and he was prepared to serve anywhere.[39] Thus, he had no compunction, for example, about applying for a command in the army which the Bourbons ordered to Spain in 1823 even though he admitted that its mission was 'to crush liberty'.[40] It was surely fortunate for his later reputation as a liberal and a nationalist that his application was turned down.

It may be argued that, to a large extent, Byrne's relative silence on the darker side of soldiering in Spain stemmed from the customary military distaste for insurgency, and its repression. Indeed so palpable was Byrne's dislike for this duty that even in his chapters on the rebellion in Ireland, as noted above, he constantly stressed the military discipline and good order maintained by the Irish rebels, in effect denying that they were insurgents. The camp at Vinegar Hill, for example, he recalled as looking like 'the bivouac of a regular French army' – a description seriously at odds with those of other eye-witnesses.[41]

For his own part, Byrne claimed throughout his own career that he had been from the beginning – precisely dated to 10 January 1797 – *not* a rebel in arms in Ireland, but a soldier of France.[42] Hence his anger when, on his retirement from the French army in 1835, he discovered that some two years' pensionable service (the years 1797-8) had been docked from his record. In truth, this made a difference of only 100 francs p.a. to the pension of 1,988 francs awarded to a *Chef de Battaillon* with over thirty years' service. None the less, the blow to Byrne's self-esteem as a professional soldier, proud of his distinguished service record, and certain that his insurgent career in Ireland was of a piece with his later soldiering in the Irish Legion led him to lodge a formal protest at this reduction:

> L'exposant, né le 20 mars 1780, entra le 10 janvier 1797 au service de la France lors de l'insurrection irlandaise evidemment provoquée, dirigée et commandée par des agens et des géneraux français. Il participa pendant les années 1797 et 1798 à cette guerre à laquelle la France attachait tant de prix et qui devint la source de si grands sacrifices. Le sort des armées n'ayant cependant pas été favourable sur ce point, les malheureux Irlandais qui avait répondu á l'appel du gouvernment français quittérent l'Irlande et vinrent en France où ils furent accueillis comme des frères.[43]

Byrne's view of the rebellion as having been 'instigated, directed and commanded by French agents and generals' was highly questionable, but even so his complaint was upheld and his campaign in Ireland was restored to his pensionable service. Curiously, he never claimed that his role in Robert Emmet's conspiracy warranted recognition for pension purposes, possibly because the Treaty of Amiens (1802-3) had been in force during his involvement with Emmet, or perhaps because the latter had always stressed that he was not acting on behalf of the French government.

Happily, Miles Byrne's relative silence on his counter-insurgency role in Spain was not replicated in his account of the more formal soldiering that he was involved in from 1803 to 1815. Prompted perhaps by W.J. MacNeven, he very quickly appears to have taken on the role of historian of the Irish Legion and, at an early stage, he began to make notes of its services and campaigns.[44] He recorded a great many biographical and service details of the Irish officers with whom he came in contact during the war years and in volumes two and three of his *Memoirs*, he presents a series of fascinating individual portraits of that striking group of men who formed the officer corps of Bonaparte's Irish Legion.[45]

Byrne did not flinch from describing the inauspicious beginnings of the Irish Legion when personality clashes, bitter rivalries and an unfortunate propensity for duelling threatened the whole enterprise. He was happiest, however, at recounting its later distinguished history when it proudly bore before it on its numerous campaigns a regimental eagle awarded by Bonaparte. Byrne loved the military life and he relished the atmosphere within the Legion. 'We were not only comrades but we lived together like brothers', he wrote, 'and this made hard service and privations often less felt than they otherwise would have been'.[46] There were compensations, of course, as well as privations. At Antwerp, though the city was under siege, there was a delightful dalliance with the aimiable Miss Sally Masterson: at Brussels there was a round of plays and masked Balls, and cake and sherry could be had; and in Spain, at the coastal resort of Gijon, Byrne spent 'an agreeable evening' with a Spanish lady whose husband was in hiding.[47]

Some diversions, however, had their piquant side. While stationed at Burgos, Byrne and his comrades had gathered together on 17 March 1809. 'The Irish abroad', he noted, 'and particularly the exiles banished from their homes, were often more enthusiastic about celebrating Saint Patrick's day than if they had been living quietly in the green Island'. Present at the dinner were Colonel Daniel O'Meara, commander of the garrison, Colonel O'Neill, whose father had commanded Walshe's regiment in the old Irish Brigade in the French service, a Prussian officer, 'a Mr Plunkett' whose father 'was the son of an Irishman born in the

Austrian states', a number of Irish officers who had served in the Irish regiments of the Spanish army and, of course, Byrne and his colleagues from the Irish Legion. Byrne found it a moving occasion:

> Thus the exiles of 1798 had the honour of entertaining at the festival of their patron saint, 'Patrick', the descendants of those of the different epochs of Ireland's sad history. What a picture an able hand might have drawn of Ireland's misfortunes, inspired by the varied and woeful histories of the ancestors of our guests![48]

Time and time again, in his account of the Irish-born officers he met, he lamented that their service had not been for Ireland. The reunion of the O'Meara twin brothers in Spain prompted the thought that this was 'another instance of the misfortune of poor Ireland: had she been allowed to govern herself these brave officers would have been an ornament to her commonwealth in place of wandering abroad to seek their fortunes'.[49] And when the former insurgent leader from Kildare, William Aylmer, now a captain in the Austrian Army, after a lapse of near sixteen years, met up with his former comrade, and present enemy, Hugh Ware, now a colonel in the Irish Legion, in 1814 at the end of the wars, Byrne mused: 'How melancholy it is to think of such brave men not having a country of their own to fight for'.[50]

In describing his campaigns in Spain, memories of the fighting in Wexford were never far from his mind. We have already noted how an animated conversation with a Spanish priest quickly turned into a disquisition on the role of the Catholic clergy of Wexford during the rebellion. Similarly, he wrote of the great disappointment among the officers of the Irish Legion that they had arrived too late in Spain to cross swords once again with their old adversary, Sir John Moore, whom they had fought against in Wexford and Wicklow in 1798. This in turn led on to a digression on the respective qualities of Moore, 'this gallant general' and of the Lord Lieutenant at the time of the 1798 rebellion, Lord Cornwallis, dubbed by Byrne 'a cold-hearted monster'.[51]

Even when Byrne recounted proudly the heroic action of individual officers such as that of his friend Captain John Allen at the capture of the fortress of Astorga (1810), Wexford was not far from his mind. Allen's company of voltigeurs (lightly armed skirmishers) had been ordered to lead the attack on a breach in the wall. Crossing two hundred yards of open ground, under the constant fire of more than 2,000 men, Allen and his 150 men successfully carried their objective, despite sustaining heavy casualties. The fortress, its defences breached, soon surrendered. It was a great victory, made all the more memorable by Irish heroism. Byrne commented that the subsequent French restraint at Astorga contrasted sharply with English indiscipline in similar situations elsewhere in Spain – which, of course, was of a piece with the rapacity of the Ancient Britons in Wexford.[52] As we shall see, even in peace-time, Byrne continued to dwell on Wexford and the rebellion.

IV

For Miles Byrne the years after 1815 were a period of danger, disappointment and frustration. In 1814, Bonaparte had conceded defeat and been exiled by the allies to Elba. However, in early 1815 he had returned in triumph only to be finally defeated at Waterloo in June of that year. Such vicissitudes called for some adroit footwork as Emperor yielded to King, King yielded to Emperor and then finally, the *fourbes* (or deceitful ones) were left exposed to public gaze when Napoleon was exiled to St Helena.

Byrne's conduct during the '100 days' was adjudged questionable (at best) and, with the standing down of the Irish Legion (Byrne blamed Castlereagh for this), he and some other Irish officers were ordered out of France. Luckily for Byrne, he had not been directly involved in Bonaparte's return ('je n'ai pris aucune part active dans le moment de l'interrègne') and, after appealing the expulsion order, he was allowed a stay of execution.[53] This gave him an opportunity to put together testimonials both to his good behaviour and to his general political outlook. For a time his prospects looked bleak and Byrne resigned himself to exile in the United States. One report to the Minister of War, dated December 1815, declared bluntly that he was 'un homme fourbe, méchant et très dangèreux: a été partisan furieux de Bonaparte et ne changera jamais. Doit être fortement surveillé quelque soit son domicile'. Another, a few months later, said he had 'mauvaises opinions' and pronounced him 'à n'être pas employé'.[54] Accordingly, he was kept under strict police surveillance throughout 1816 and 1817, but the reports on him eventually conceded that he had kept himself to himself since 1815. This report was dated February 1817:

> Il paraît être de moeurs douces et d'une conduite tranquille. Les seules personnel qu'il fréquente sont un garde ... un officier de la Garde Royale et deux professeurs du Collège des Irlandais. Ces deux derniers sont ses compatriots ... Il passe ordinairement ses soirées aux variétés ou à l'opera comique.[55]

Ironically, Byrne's chief enemy in the French government was none

other than General Henry Clarke, Duc de Feltre, of Irish Jacobite ances-
try, former friend of Theobald Wolfe Tone, and now Minister of War
under the Bourbons.[56] There is no adequate explanation for de Feltre's
hostility towards Miles Byrne: he may genuinely have believed that
Byrne was in fact 'un buonapartiste enragé' – or he may have been, as
Byrne claimed, simply vindictive towards him.[57]

However, Miles Byrne had several friends who were prepared to
intercede on his behalf. Lawless and Ware from the Irish Legion wrote in
his support – 'bon et brave officier', 'serviteur fidèle et dévoué' – and it is
likely that Edward Lewins, former United Irish envoy in Paris, and now
moving high in the Bourbon court also added his voice to those calling
for leniency.[58]

The most influential figure to intervene on Byrne's behalf was
undoubtedly the Prince de Broglie, vice-president of the Chamber of
Deputies. A friend of Byrne's from Dublin, Andrew O'Reilly, had pro-
cured Byrne a letter of introduction to the Prince from the Prince's
brother, l'Abbé de Broglie, and Byrne hurriedly arranged an audience.
The Prince, a former diplomat during the Empire, was impressed with
Byrne and he had de Feltre cancel the exclusion order. Byrne was now
free to stay in France, and he took out naturalisation papers in August
1817.[59]

Miles Byrne had ended the war with the rank of captain, having seen
almost all of those who had enlisted with him in 1803 move ahead. He
was desperately unlucky not to have been promoted *Chef de Bataillon*
before Bonaparte's defeat. Nominated to that rank on the field of battle
at Goldberg in 1813, and reaffirmed at Anvers in 1814, he had actually
gone to Paris to receive his promotion in February 1815: but in the confusion of the '100 days' he never got his *brèvet*.[60] As we have seen, in the
vengeful atmosphere of the Bourbon restoration, Byrne was fortunate to
be let remain in France and his hard luck story got short shrift. He was
put 'en non-activité' with a pension of 900 francs, 'the miserable half-pay
of a captain', and this continued for more than twelve years.[61]

Miles Byrne found it difficult to make ends meet on his niggardly
pension as a half-pay captain. Admittedly, he knew the city of Paris quite
well from his brief and penniless sojourn there in 1803; at that time he
had frequented the London Coffee House in the Rue Jacob and the Café
de la Routarde in the Palais Royale where the English newspapers were
available; and he had been friendly with many of the United Irishmen,
notably William James MacNeven and Thomas Addis Emmet, who had
thronged the city then.[62] Paris during the Bourbon restoration was, however, rather a different matter and Byrne cannot have been comfortable
with the degree of surveillance by the authorities to which he was sub-

jected. None the less, during his enforced idleness after 1815 he cultivated a wide social circle. Edward Lewins and his son, Lawrence, were
friends of Byrne and he often dined with them. Byrne visited Edward
shortly before he died and found him reading Wolfe Tone's *Memoirs*,
recently published in Washington, and commenting 'what a true
Irishman Tone was!' Edward Lewins' funeral in 1827 was the occasion
for a turn-out of 'all the Irish exiles then in Paris'.[63]

In addition, Byrne counted Dr McMahon, physician to the Collège
des Irlandais and l'Abbé Lynch, librarian there, as firm friends. In fact,
Byrne was actively involved in the defence of the Collège des Irlandais
against an attempted take-over by St Patrick's College, Maynooth in the
1820s.[64] It is likely that he attended some lectures there. Certainly, he was
an avid attender at the public lectures in other colleges in Paris, notably
the Collège du Plessis: he mentions hearing lectures by Guizot, Thénard,
Villemain, Cousin and Lacretelle. He was thrilled when the Irish
Catholic activist, Dr Thomas Drumgoole, en route from Rome and in
Byrne's company in Paris, wrote in protest at Lacretelle's encomium in a
lecture on Elizabeth I's reign. Drumgoole did his work so well that when
Lacretelle returned to this topic, Elizabeth was 'painted out worse, if
possible, than Cromwell, for her monstrous cold-blooded murders in
Ireland'.[65] Moreover, Byrne's references to the early eighteenth-century
picaresque novel by Lesage, *Gil Blas*, his excursion to Rousseau's last
residence at Erménonville, his comment on the novel *Captain Rock*, his
fondness for the exile poetry of Thomas Campbell, his fluent Spanish,
and his visit to ancient Greek ruins while campaigning in that country, all
testify to a cultured mind far removed from the stereotype of the ignorant soldier, and perhaps not to be expected in one who had taken up
arms at a tender age.[66]

On occasion, he could be found reading the English newspapers in
the Trois Frères in the Palais Royal, or meeting friends in Mrs Putland's
Hotel, Place Vendôme.[67] We catch a glimpse of him at a dinner party for
thirty guests in 1824: 'we spent a jovial evening, returning "quietly" as
Irishmen, half seas over, to our homes at midnight'.[68] And there were further dinner parties with David Baillie Warden the American consul in
Paris, and former United Irishman, and with Robert Carthy of
Birchgrove, yet another former United Irish leader from Wexford, then
visiting Paris.[69] At one dinner party he met a daughter of Hunter Gowan,
his nemesis of 1798.[70] In the mid-1820s there were also week-ends excur-
sions into the countryside in the company of John Prat Winter, a rich
merchant from Meath who with his large family had taken up residence
in Paris.[71] Once Byrne acted as a second in a duel.[72]

Furthermore, he was in demand to escort visiting Irish worthies through Paris: he took care of Mr Harvey, the editor of the *Freeman's Journal*, on his visit to Paris in 1818; he was much in the company of the former United Irishman, now successful merchant, Mr William Murphy and his family in 1824; and he dined with Mr Cramer, an Irish Protestant landlord, and his wife on their visit in 1825.[73] He was always willing to do a favour for his compatriots, especially those from Wexford: in 1825, on foot of a request from a Mrs Ryan of Wexford (possibly a relative) he was able to help her grandson, Andrew Kennedy, enlist in the French army.[74] Again in 1826, 'Mr James Power, his mother and sisters came to France and brought me a letter of introduction' and he was able to facilitate them.[75]

In truth, Ireland, Wexford, and the 1798 rebellion were never far from his mind, though he was never to return home.[76] On one occasion, he agonised over attending a St Patrick's Day dinner at which the guest of honour was to be Thomas Moore, 'Ireland's great poet'. The problem arose because the Duke of Wellington's nephew, William Wellesley-Pole, was to preside and Byrne, a serving French officer (even if *en non-activité*) 'who had fought the English in Ireland in 1798 and in Spain and Portugal in 1809-10 and 11', felt he had no business there, sitting down 'with the heroes of Waterloo'. The recollection of Tom Moore and Moore's poem, 'The Vale of Avoca', conjured up another, more poignant, memory:

> That country, the 'Vale of Avoca', was the home of my dear mother's ancestors, the Grahams, and her birthplace, and where I, when a youngster, spent many happy days, roaming on the banks of the Avoca, and in the Cherry orchard of [*sic*, near?] the wooden bridge.

Perhaps fortified by this maternal memory, he pocketed his misgivings and attended the dinner, though the occasion was marred by a row over a toast proposed to Thomas Reynolds (a leading '98 informer), and a duel was threatened.[77]

Miles Byrne supplemented his meagre income by undertaking some commissions for those Irish who lived beyond Paris, and the hospitality of his friends was greatly appreciated.[78] Frank Thorp, a wealthy Dublin financier then resident in Paris, kept a good table and, as Byrne recorded, 'when we happened to meet in our walks he frequently begged me if I had no other engagement to come and share their family dinner'.[79] He lived modestly, even frugally, in Paris and his several changes of lodgings in the 1820s are probably an index of his financial difficulties.

Disappointingly, his many pleas for his promotion to *Chef de Bataillon* to be confirmed – or even to be brought back onto active service – were ignored. He was turned down for the Garde Royale and was refused a command in the French expedition to Spain in 1823. Byrne blamed English intrigue for these setbacks to his career and there was much in this charge. He applied for the award of Chevalier de St Louis in 1821 and, though de Broglie supported his claim, he appears not to have received this award, or the modest boost to his income which it would have meant.[80]

Finally, in 1828 his luck turned, and at the age of forty-eight he was recalled to active service in the French expedition to help the Greeks in their war of independence against the Turks. His friend from the old days in Spain, Colonel O'Neill, the son of the last commander of Walshe's regiment and now something in the French War Office, got him a command. The protests of the English diplomat, Sir Charles Stuart, were ignored: Lawrence Lewins, the son of Byrne's friend, had great influence at the court of Charles X, and Byrne's appointment to General Maison's staff (and that of Colonel William Corbet, another ex-United Irishman, to the expeditionary force) were confirmed.[81] Dr Daniel Halliday, a friend and benefactor, then living in Dieppe, kindly sent Byrne 1,000 francs to get himself kitted out for his staff command, and he embarked soon after for the Morea peninsula in Greece.[82]

If only because he finally received his *brèvet* as *Chef de Bataillon* for this campaign, Miles Byrne would have had vivid memories of his service in Greece. But in addition, he had closely followed events there for some years and was ardently pro-Greek. He greatly admired Byron who had died in 1824 at Missolonghi fighting on behalf of the Greeks, and he had grieved for Arthur Winter, the son of his friend, who had also perished while aiding them.[83] There can be no doubt but that he saw marked resemblances between the Greek situation and that of Ireland. Equally, that he regarded the expedition to Greece against the 'cruel Turks' as in many respects a surrogate for his longed-for expedition to Ireland against 'the bloodthirsty English taskmasters'.[84]

The Greek revolt against the Turks had been characterised by extraordinary savagery involving the massacre or enslavement of tens of thousands of men, women and children. The Tsar had ordered his army to come to the aid of his co-religionists in Greece and, fearing that Russia might have further designs on the Turkish empire, France and Britain had entered into an alliance with the Tsar in order to keep an eye on him. The campaign was a resounding success: the Turkish fleet was destroyed at Navarino, the Egyptian army fighting for the Turks was forced to withdraw, and Greek independence was secured. For his part, Byrne was

Miles Byrne of Monaseed, at
the age of 79; from the original
by E. Yatel, in the President's
collection of historical portraits;
courtesy of the President of
Ireland

finally promoted Chef de Bataillon in September 1830 and he ended the
war as commander of Morea Castle.

Undoubtedly, Miles Byrne had planned a lengthy account of his last
foreign expedition but, in the event, by the time he died in 1862 he had
only composed some 40 pages on it, compared to nearly 1,000 pages
devoted to Ireland, Spain and France during the years 1798 to 1828.[85]
Despite this disparity, there are grounds for arguing that the campaign in
Greece had a greater impact on his thinking about Ireland than that in
Spain, and that had he lived he would have developed detailed compar-
isons between the Greek and Irish situations.

The role of religion among the insurgents, in both Greece and Spain,
and the part played by foreign assistance (ditto) might have figured on
his agenda in this regard. Already in volume one of his *Memoirs* he had
begun to draw some lessons for Ireland from his experience of the Greek
War of Independence. In what appears to be a lengthy digression, but is
in fact a sober, if sombre, assessment of the collapse of the Irish rebellion
in Wexford, he compared Cornwallis to the Egyptian leader Ibrahim
Pasha (to the former's disfavour) and went on to comment on the role
that atrocity and reprisal had played in the war in Greece. Byrne noted
that Ibrahim Pasha, charged by the Turks with crushing the Greek insurrection, had issued protections to all those who would agree to return
peacefully to their homes. This tactic had an effect (as had Cornwallis's

similar tactic in Ireland) and support for the independence struggle noticeably ebbed. The response of the Greek generals to this setback was to capture as many of Pasha's soldiers as they could, mutilate them and send them back to him. Enraged at this, Pasha unleashed his army on the civilian population with such spectacular cruelty that the people flocked, once again, to the generals in the mountains. Byrne proceeded to draw the stark lesson:

> From this moment all the world could see that though Ibrahim had a disciplined army, he never could pacify or conquer a people capable of making any sacrifice under heaven to shake off the monstrous Turkish yoke. I mention all this to show how dearly liberty must be bought when there is not a levy en masse in the first instance to crush and annihilate the cruel taskmasters and tyrants who are in possession of the strongholds. Had a simultaneous rising taken place in Ireland in the month of May 1798, as it had been agreed on by the Irish Directory and Lord Edward Fitzgerald, what a mass of misery might have been prevented! Torrents of blood might not then have been shed in vain! Or had even ten counties of the provinces of Munster and Leinster commenced the war at the same time, and with the same success as the county of Wexford, England had then no forces to resist so powerful a mass of people resolved to shake off her yoke ... We wanted an able general in chief, or in other words an honest dictator whose orders could never be disobeyed under pain of death, as on the prompt execution of them depended the success of our holy undertaking ... If we had had a general commanding in Wexford on the 21st of June, of the stamp of the Greek generals I have mentioned, he would no doubt have dispatched Lord Kingsborough [the leading rebel prisoner] and his fellow English prisoners to the English headquarters with their ears and noses cut off, the moment he learnt that all our sick and wounded were burned in the hospital at Enniscorthy by orders of general Lake.

Miles Byrne's point, born of his experience of the war in Greece (and also, though unstated, of the war in Spain) was that moderation in the commanders, a willingness to negotiate, to talk, to accept 'protections' would only prove futile and ultimately fatal. If the rebel leaders – such as Bagenal Harvey, John Hay, Cornelius Grogan, Philip Roche and the others – had conducted themselves like the Greek generals, had realised that they could never make terms for themselves or indeed anyone else, then, Byrne remarked grimly, 'they would at least have saved the citizens of Wexford the hideous spectacle of their heads being placed on pikes over the public edifices of the town and there left to bleach and wither into dust'.[86]

Miles Byrne left the French army in 1835. His wife, Fanny Horner, whom he had married shortly after his retirement, claimed that he was 'in perfect health' at this time, though his army report from 1831 describes him as having 'la poitrine faible et la voix usée' and concluded that he was not 'en état de faire campagne'.[87] Some leisurely garrison duty with his regiment, the 56th Infantry, at Nantes and then at Paris followed; and there was a short spell on more active duty in Brittany where there had been some royalist unrest at the government of Louis-Philippe.

On his retirement, Byrne lived as before, quietly and modestly, and he continued to enjoy a wide circle of friends. His best friend from his army days was the Piedmontese, Gaetano Viaris who, like Byrne, had left his home many years before to fight in Bonaparte's campaigns. 'Between these two arose a friendship made up of a sympathy of habits, feelings and opinions such as is known only to military comrades and which never declined till poor Viaris was no more', so Byrne wrote in this obituary of his friend.[88] He also wrote an obituary of the widow of General William Lawless of the Irish Legion and this was published in the *Nation* (Dublin) in 1854, and he may have contributed occasional pieces to this paper.[89] In 1840, he compiled a lengthy, and highly critical, report on Gustave de Beaumont's *Irlande, sociale, politique et religieuse* in 1840, for he claimed (rightly) that de Beaumont had misrepresented the whole affair of the 1798 rebellion. However, Byrne decided against publishing this at the time for de Beaumont 'was the first French gentleman of station who for a long time had written on the sufferings of Ireland under her taskmasters'.[90]

For the most part, however, he busied himself in getting his notes and correspondence in order so that the could compile his memoirs accurately. 'A mass of letters' was put at his disposal by General Lawless's son and by Arthur Barker, the son of the Wexford insurgent, and a close friend for many years in Paris.[91] There was support for his project from Colonel O'Neill who at one time had planned his own history of the Irish Legion, but who was forced to give up through ill-health.[92] It is probable that W.J. Fitzpatrick, the noted and prolific historian of the 1790s and the biographer of O'Connell, lent his encouragement.[93] The publication of Mathew O'Conor's *Military History of the Irish Nation, comprising a Memoir of the Irish Brigade in the service of France* (Dublin, 1845) may also have spurred Byrne on by leading him to reflect on his career as one of the nineetenth-century 'Wild Geese'.

Work on his memoirs proceeded extremely slowly: it might even be claimed that he was at work on them for nearly forty years and they bear some of the signs of emendation, interpolation, and perhaps pentimento. At the time of his death in 1862 the most finished section of his memoirs was the first volume dealing with events in Ireland from 1798 to 1803. In 1854, Byrne had written to W.J. Fitzpatrick telling him that 'I have made notes of the principal events and transactions that came within my knowledge during the insurrection of 1798 as well as that of 1803', but he went on to doubt if the present time was propitious for their publication. 'I trust a time may come' he wrote, 'when the publication of such documents will be encouraged. They will show the efforts and sacrifices that were made to procure the independence of Ireland'.[94] A re-issue of that volume of Miles Byrne's *Memoirs* concerning Ireland during the years 1798 to 1803 would afford a new generation another opportunity of passing its own judgement on his work.

APPENDIX

1. Statement concerning Miles Byrne's activities in Wexford in 1798 (N.D. c.1805)

Miles Byrne agé de 25 ans, natif du Comté de Wexford en Irlande. Dans l'insurrection de 1798, il commandait à un corps contentant 1,500 hommes nommé le Monaseed Corps et qui se distinquait beaucoup dans les mois de mai, juin et juillet contre l'ennemi. Apres la défaite des insurgés, vu leur état dépourvu, il se rétirait dans les montagnes avec le débris de son corps montant à peu près à 500 hommes où il faisait la petite guerre contre les Anglais même après la soumission du Géneral Humbert. Il ne s'est jamais rendu, mais au commencement de l'hiver il laissait échapper chez eux son monde peu à peu et il se cachait lui même à Dublin où il vivait en secret jusqu' à ce qu'il parût offrir une autre occasion de secouer le joug anglais. Il jouit pleinement de la confiance de ceux qui se tiennent prêts à agir en Irlande et on l'a choisi pour l'expédier en France. Il a une très grande influence sur le peuple qui le connait dans le Comté de Wexford et dans la capitale même.

(Byrne dossier, Vincennes)

[Miles Byrne, 25 years of age, native of County Wexford, Ireland. In the insurrection of 1798 he commanded a corps containing 1,500 men called the Monaseed Corps and which distinquished itself greatly in the months of May, June and July against the enemy. Following the defeat of the insurgents, seeing their destitute state, he withdrew to the mountains with the remnants of his corps, almost 500 men, where he carried on a guerilla war against the English, even after the submission of General Humbert. He was never taken, but at the beginning of winter, he allowed his men gradually to return home and he went into hiding in Dublin where he lived secretly until another opportunity offered to throw off the English yoke. He enjoyed the full confidence of those who held themselves ready to act in Ireland and he was chosen to bring the news to France. He has a great influence with the people whom he knows in County Wexford and in the capital itself.]

1798 Claimed for Catholics: Father Kavanagh, Fenians and the Centenary Celebrations

Anna Kinsella

Many factors contribute to the popular perception of the Wexford rebellion of 1798, as the provoked response of a downtrodden people to insufferable atrocities committed in the name of law and order. Such interpretations resulted from the fact that many of the early writers were apologists for the outbreak, but it is in the writings of Patrick Kavanagh that the rebellion received its distinctly Catholic character. His *Popular History of the Insurrection of 1798*, first published in about the year 1870, quickly became the popularly accepted account of the rebellion. It characterised the rising as a struggle for 'Faith and Fatherland'; the response of a Catholic people to an oppressive reign of terror by the politically motivated Protestant Orange Society.[1]

I

Patrick Kavanagh was born in Wexford in March 1838. Twenty-one years later, he entered the Franciscan Order at Capranica, forty miles from Rome, where he received the name Fidelis. As a novice in Italy, Kavanagh witnessed the assault of the Italian nationalists on the Papal States and these memories of the Carbonari made a lasting impression on the young cleric.[2] He was ordained priest on 15 April 1865 and returned to Ireland in the following year to serve in counties Kerry and Cork, strongholds of Fenianism.

While the rising of 1867 had failed, and most of the leaders were imprisoned, Fenianism continued as a significant factor in Irish politics and efforts were made in 1870 to re-organise the Fenian society.[3] In that year too, the outbreak of the Franco-Prussian war raised hopes in Ireland that England might be drawn in, thus providing the ever-awaited opportunity for Ireland to strike a blow for freedom.[4] In addition, the 1870s witnessed the emergence of the Home Rule movement which presented the real possibility of a predominantly Protestant parliament in Dublin. Against this background Father Kavanagh, published *The*

Father Patrick
F. Kavanagh

Wexford Rebellion. It was a small book, of 120 pages, in which the author narrated the events of the 1798 insurrection in Wexford as told to him by survivors and those who had heard it from the people involved. The insurrection was given a blatantly religious dimension as Kavanagh set out to prove that there was no conflict between Irish Nationalism and Catholicism, and that in the hour of need it was the priest who stood by the Irish people.

Kavanagh tread a fine line between physical force republicanism on the one hand and constitutional politics on the other. He consciously distanced the Wexford rebellion from the planned revolution of the United Irish Society. Nevertheless, while 'the people of Wexford, in the main, had kept aloof from the conspiracy of the United Irishmen ... this did not save them from the fury of persecution'. Moreover, the United Irishmen were blamed for creating a climate of political intrigue which exposed innocent people to the excesses of the violent behaviour of the Orange Society; holding responsibility for provoking this, they had failed to fulfil their obligations to the people.[5]

Nevertheless, he acknowledged that the United Irishmen were well organised in some districts of County Wexford, especially in the barony of Shelmalier.[6] This view was subsequently modified in the centenary edition of his book in which he stated that 'the organisation existed in the county for a considerable time before the outbreak of the insurrection, but made little progress, owing both to the opposition offered to it by the priests as a secret society, and to the peculiar character of the Wexford people, who had always been averse to secret societies.[7]

Kavanagh explained the Protestant involvement on the rebel side as deriving from the fact that these were liberal gentlemen who simply desired to live in peace with their Catholic fellow countrymen and who wished to see them restored to their civil and religious liberty.[8] As a contrast, the Orange Society was shown as allying with the 'foreign oppressors' while there were also loyalist Catholics who offered their services against their countrymen and co-religionists.[9] Father Kavanagh's principal concern however, was not the United Irishmen, but the Fenians of his own time; it was to them his argument was addressed.

The Fenian challenge had first been addressed by Cardinal Cullen in 1864. In a series of pastorals, he argued that the moral law could not condone an oath-bound society which demanded blind allegiance to unknown leaders.[10] His condemnation of Fenianism continued, but not until 1868 was it decided to petition Rome for an explicit condemnation of the society.[11] The publication of that decree produced an angry reaction from Fenian sympathisers in Ireland. Yet, this did not deter Cullen who, in his pastoral read on 1 May 1870, denounced the Fenians as 'men without principle or religion'.[12]

Kavanagh, fearing that such harsh condemnation might alienate the people from the clergy, chose this time to publish his history of *The Wexford Rebellion*. Kavanagh was clearly in a dilemma. In pointing to the priests as leaders of the Wexford rebellion he identified with the grievances of the Fenians. Yet, he remained in a difficult position, having to publicly denounce the Fenians, while personally sympathising with their separatist aspirations.[13] Kavanagh's answer was to distance the excellent character of the men who join secret societies from the societies themselves.

II

In 1873, the Protestant lawyer Isaac Butt founded the Home Rule League and by the Autumn of that year large numbers of priests had begun to support the movement publicly.[14] It is not clear whether Kavanagh supported the early Home Rule programme, but he certainly favoured separatist nationalism in later years, arguing that 'what England gives she can take away' and that 'if Ireland prospered under Home Rule England would take it away'.[15]

In 1874, the publication of the second edition of Kavanagh's book, this time entitled *A popular history of the Insurrection of 1798*, coincided with the return to Parliament of fifty-nine Irish Home Rulers led by Butt. The rhetoric of '98 would add an extra dimension to the demand for Home Rule. This second edition was larger than the first and reflected the author's perusal of the works of earlier writers, including Hay, Gordon, Cloney, Teeling, Plowden, O'Kelly, Barrington and Byrne. Nevertheless, Kavanagh chose to ignore Miles Byrne's statement that 1797 was a year of great political activity, when thousands daily had taken the United Irishmen's oath. He also ignored Byrne's account of the funeral of an United Irishman in the Gorey area, which was attended by vast crowds organised in sections and marching order, which attracted the attention of the local magistrate Hunter Gowan and alerted him to the possibility of a conspiracy in the country.[16]

Similarly, Kavanagh made no mention of the work of Brother Luke Cullen (1793–1859) or of Dr Madden. Both Miles Byrne and Luke Cullen were in no doubt that Wexford was organised in '98. Byrne asserted that in the Gorey district the United Irishmen were simply waiting for the word which was expected to come through Robert Graham or Anthony Perry. Likewise, Cullen claimed that the people of the Blackwater area, were led by George Sparks, a Protestant and a known United Irishman, into the village in the hope of meeting with Edward Fitzgerald of Newpark who, on that night, was arrested along with Beauchamp Bagenal Harvey. At Ballinamonabeg the United Irishmen were meeting in the public house of Jeremiah Kavanagh (Father Kavanagh's grandfather) while at Boolavogue the men gathered on the turf bank until the decision was reached by Father John Murphy and Tom Donovan that, being no longer safe to be there, they should return to their homes.

It is possible however, that Kavanagh was unaware of Cullen's letters, published under the pen-name of *A Milesian* in the *Telegraph* and *Catholic Telegraph* from 1856 to 1858, since he was in Italy from 1859 until 1866, the year in which the *Catholic Telegraph* ceased publication. With regard to Byrne, Kavanagh admitted the *Memoirs* were 'very interesting', but concluded that it is 'inaccurate in some important statements' and doubted that Miles Byrne, at seventeen years of age, would be chosen as a leader of the Wexford pikemen.[17]

Byrne had placed the events of 1798 in a firm political context, claiming that the United Irishmen and Presbyterians (whether sworn or not) were all republicans. The French, he claimed, were coming not for conquest but to afford the the Irish an occasion to declare their right to self government. According to Byrne, the country possessed the resources necessary for this great undertaking;

the church property becoming immediately the property of the state; and the estates of all those who should emigrate, or remain in the English army, fighting against their country being confiscated, the revenue arising from these funds would have been employed to provide for and defray all the expenses necessary for the defence and independence of the country.[18]

Such analysis ran contrary to Kavanagh's interpretation of 1798 as a rebellion for 'Faith and Fatherland'. Similarly, Kavanagh regarded as 'inaccurate' statements in Byrne's *Memoirs* relating to the strength of the United Irishmen in County Wexford.

Kavanagh believed 'it would be contrary to truth to say that there were no United Irishmen in the county of Wexford but by every state-ment worthy of credit that has ever appeared, their numbers were com-paratively fewer in this than in any other county in Ireland'. The people, he claimed, were driven to despair by the extreme measures of the Government:

> [when it] seemed plain that no man, however innocent, could deem himself safe; when to be a 'Papist' or even a liberal Protest-ant was a crime that sufficed to bring down destruction on his head ... It was in these circumstances they resolved upon resistance and then began to take the oath in great numbers.[19]

On the other hand, he acknowledges that the Wexford delegates of United Irishmen happened to be assembled in the public house of Jeremiah Kavanagh (his grandfather) at the time of the outbreak in Oulart. Nevertheless, this was not a planned Insurrection; 'the people were roused to madness by an oppressive reign of terror by the Orange Society' and 'it was in this crisis ... that ... a man was found, fearless enough ... to raise the standard of revolt'.[20]

III

This was Father John Murphy, the Catholic curate of Kilcormick, 'who had opposed the organisation of the United Irishmen, not from lack of patriotism, but because being a secret society he deemed it unlawful'. Kavanagh portrayed Father Murphy in an heroic mould: 'Well might those bold peasants accept with joy their proffered leader, for he had been cast by nature in the mould of those who lead men to victory'.[21] This heroic ideal found permanent expression in the bronze 1798 memo-rial erected in the Market Square in Enniscorthy.

The Oliver Sheppard statue in Enniscorthy

The Enniscorthy monument consists of two figures; the larger is a priest, Father John Murphy of Boolavogue, whose right hand rests on the shoulder of a young rebel holding a pike in one hand and a sword in the other. The leadership of Father John is emphasised by the outstretched left arm and hand in pointing position and the unfurled flag attached to the pike has a unifying effect on the two figures. A rosary hangs from the pocket of the priest. Turpin has interpreted the monument's representation of 1798 as:

> a morally righteous insurrection by a devout Catholic people, led by the Catholic clergy fighting for their rights against an alien

oppressor ... The monument thus compresses the history of the Wexford 1798 Rebellion ... into a single idea. This idea had more to do with the contemporary alliance of the Catholic Church and the Irish Parliamentary Party on the politics of Home Rule ... than with the 1798 Rebellion with its strong echoes of the French Revolution.[22]

Father Murphy became a towering figure in the history of the Wexford Insurrection. He was already the hero of early street ballads, some of which were preserved in writing as early as 1844 but Kavanagh's history played no small part in the development of his heroic stature. He described Murphy as 'a kind, zealous and true Irish priest, who had won the highest honours of scholarship in a foreign university yet had ever lived among his humble flock as one of themselves ... Hitherto he had been their leader in peace, now they should follow him in the struggle for freedom.'[23]

Significantly, Miles Byrne had shared this admiration and affection for Murphy:

> Father John having decided that they had better die courageously in the field than be butchered in their houses ... all cried out that they were determined to follow his advice and to do whatever he ordered ... Thus he became general-in-chief 'provisionally' ... Would to God he had been confirmed in this rank all through.[24]

Clearly the priest as leader was the subject of Kavanagh's thesis and the leadership of Father John was bolstered by other priest leaders. Father Michael Murphy, Kavanagh claimed, had from the outset been strongly opposed to armed resistance on the grounds that it could not succeed and was therefore unlawful. Nevertheless, if the people were to attempt resistance Father Michael had promised to 'go with the people' and it was in fulfilment of this promise that he joined the insurgents on Kilthomas Hill.[25] Father Michael, incidentally was Kavanagh's maternal grand-uncle.

Kavanagh commended the virtues and personal attributes of all the priests who took part in the rebellion, judging them as well fitted to be popular leaders. The reality as shown by recent studies is that 'of the eighty-five priests in the county in 1798 only eleven played an active role in the Insurrection and many of the remaining seventy-four 'were either active loyalists or kept a very low profile'.[26] By contrast, Garret Byrne, Thomas Cloney, William Barker and John Kelly are described simply as brave men while the Commander-in-Chief, Bagenal Harvey, was dismissed in mostly negative terms.[27] Kavanagh failed to mention that any of these were United Irishmen.

IV

In March 1875, the Fenian John Mitchel was returned unopposed as Member of Parliament for County Tipperary.[28] However, his health was poor and he lived for a mere eight days after the controversial election. Few people were allowed to visit him but Father Kavanagh was favoured, because he was the descendant of a '98 pikeman and was regarded as something of a rebel himself.[29] Kavanagh, who met him in Cork, later recalled how Mitchel liked to speak of '98 and was a great admirer of Father John Murphy, 'the chief leader' in that famous fight for freedom.[30]

The Fenians remained to be convinced of the value of constitutional politics and many of their number became involved in measures to revive the memory of 1798. In 1875, the earliest known monument to commemorate the dead of '98 was erected in St Mary's cemetery, Newtownbarry, now Bunclody. Two years later, arising out of a meeting in Aungier St., Dublin, a commemoration of '98 was held in Boolavogue.

On 10 May 1877, an advertisement was displayed extensively throughout Dublin city proclaiming the first celebration of the anniversary of the Battle of Oulart. Published by a committee of the '98 Club, this notice invited the nationalists of Ireland to co-operate in honouring the memory of the 'Heroes of '98', on Whit Sunday, 20 May 1877. Amongst the invited speakers, the poster listed C.J. Kickham, Charles Stewart Parnell, M.P., J.G. Biggar, M.P., J. Sarsfield-Casey, Charles Guilfoyle-Doran and other prominent nationalists.

The Oulart demonstration did not, however, reach the hoped for heights of success. It is not clear whether those invited to speak attended, while police reports to Dublin Castle stated that 'at any time during the march there were not five hundred people present'; most of those, the report continued, were attracted by the 'music and gaudy uniform of the Dundalk Emmet Band'. The informants were satisfied that the hearts of the people were not with the nationalists.[31]

The '98 Club, comprised of young men from County Wexford residing in Dublin, was not to be deterred and decided to erect a memorial cross to the men of '98 at Boolavogue.[32] Sculptor John Cullen, of Enniscorthy, was commissioned to make a twenty-four feet high cross at a cost of one hundred and twenty pounds. However, when the parish priests of Ferns and Boolavogue refused to allow the monument to be

The '98 Committee's outing to Kilmore Quay. The Wexford Borough Committee
embarked on an excursion to Kilmore with their great banner to draw the viewers
attention. The Hon. Treasurer J.J. Stafford is enthroned in front alongside Ben
Hughes in sailor's cap. The gentleman in the hard hat second from the right is
Edward O'Connor of Selskar.

erected in the church yard at Boolavogue, it was decided to place it at
Ballytracy, a short distance away.

Special trains arrived in Ferns from Dublin and Wexford for the
unveiling ceremony which took place at the end of September. A proces-
sion of thousands of people, headed by Wexford's St John's Independent
Band made its way from Ferns, through the Harrow to Ballytracy Lane.
They were joined by the Bricklayers' Brass Band and St James' Fife and
Drum Band from Dublin and the York Street Fife and Drum Band from
Kingstown had travelled to take part in the ceremonies.

On the previous evening a priest of the parish instructed a young lad
to remove the covering of cloth and garlands from the memorial cross.
He refused but another boy was found who performed the task for a
sum of two shillings. There was consternation when the procession
arrived and found the monument uncovered. Undeterred, Charles
Guilfoyle Doran of Queenstown took the chair and in an impassioned
address reminded the crowd that the same cause which induced Father
Murphy to take up arms still survived. Whenever the time came for their
redress, he continued, the means would be the same as those of which
Father Murphy set them the example. Doran concluded by associating

these grievances with the land question. 'Were they content', he asked, 'that these things should go on for ever?' The answer was 'No!' and he bade them bide their time until Providence put them in a position when England could no longer afford to despise them. There were loud cheers and, and appealing to their patriotism, he declared his hope that as long as the cross existed no one would see it without praying for the Heroes who had fallen or vowing to imitate their example of Christian fortitude and patriotism.

The *Wexford Independent* reported that the demonstration was large despite the exhortations of the priests to their parishioners to stay aloof from the 'rag, tag and bobtail' of Dublin, but emphasised that it be taken as a representative. Nevertheless, the newspaper acknowledged the strength of the '98 Clubs in its admission that there were few there who were not members. At Ferns however, the public houses remained closed and 'the fasting crowds, having knocked in vain for something to eat', returned to Dublin. The reporter commended the conduct of the people of Ferns and their obedience to their pastor but remarked that their loss in money in keeping their shops closed was considerable. He asked 'Is it not time to stop this useless and senseless revival of old memories? and continued 'it is in the power of the clergy to do so if they took the matter up properly ... Some clergy have spoken while the rest remained silent.'[33]

V

In the general election of 1880, the Home Rule party met some of its most violent opposition in County Wexford. Not even Parnell could not secure a hearing and was assaulted with a battery of rotten eggs by the supporters of Keyes O'Clery, a Papal Chevalier at Enniscorthy on 28 March. Father Nicholas Murphy, chairman of the Chevalier's organising committee, asked at the same meeting: 'here in the shadow of Vinegar Hill is it to be told that the priests ... the bishop and the people of Wexford cannot select their own candidate?' O'Clery, in fact, was heavily defeated at the polls by Parnell's candidate.[34]

The subsequent election of 1884 brought a new edition of Kavanagh's *History of the Insurrection of 1798*. Since many members of the Home Rule party were Protestant, Kavanagh feared the prospect of a parliament in which they would have a large say. He viewed the Orange Society as 'a political faction inveterately hostile to the rights of the majority of his fellow-countrymen' and he held that England's policy was to prevent any improvement in the condition of the Irish people.[35]

'Creed and nationality', he declared, 'had been pressed in the same vice of oppression ... and ... welded into one. The blows directed at the Catholic struck the Nationalist and vice versa' and thus the terms Catholic and Nationalist had become synonymous.[36]

Kavanagh remained a separatist. He rejected Daniel O'Connell's view that 'the freedom of a nation is not to be purchased by the shedding of a single drop of human blood', but he agreed that 'peaceful means would be wiser'. There were, he argued, three conditions before the sword could lawfully be unsheathed: the wrongs endured must be intolerable: there must exist no rational hope of redressing these wrongs by peaceful agitation and there must exist a fair probability of success in the case of armed resistance.[37] Father Kavanagh sought an autonomous Catholic nation but, although a separatist, he was well aware of the folly it would be, 'to twist the lion's tail when your head is in its mouth'. In the absence of an appropriate opportunity, he believed that pacifist resistance should be offered. In this spirit he mounted an anti-recruitment drive during the Boer War.

Accordingly, Kavanagh continued to denounce the efforts of the Fenians because of the futility and dangers of secret societies. Yet, at the same time, he distrusted the type of parliament which the Irish party was attempting to secure for Ireland. Nevertheless, he acknowledged that 'the inhabitants of any country have as well founded a right to possess and govern that country as any individual in a free country has to the posses-sion of his own house or to the government of his own household'.[38]

VI

The fall and death of Parnell (1891) and the split in the Irish Parlia-mentary Party brought morale in Irish politics to an all time low. Yet during this period the Fenians chose the centenary of 1798 as an oppor-tune occasion to unite all shades of nationalist political opinion. This idea originated in America with William Lyman, leader of Clan na Gael and founder of the Irish National Brotherhood (INB).[39] The plans, however, were taken over in Dublin by the IRB who supported Lyman's opponent John Devoy, and who worked under the auspices of the Young Ireland League.[40]

The cultural societies of the 1890s played a significant role in the cen-tenary movement. In the early 1890s the Leinster Literary Society was founded by Arthur Griffith who later in 1905 founded Sinn Féin. One of the early members was William Rooney, a founder member of the Gaelic League, who after internal dissensions and a split in the Leinster

Literary Society, established a separate Celtic Literary Society to which Griffith transferred. John O'Leary, a Young Irelander, who occupied a position of prominence in the IRB of the 1860s, was one of the sponsors of the new Society. At a meeting of the Celtic Literary Society on 18 September 1891, at which O'Leary presided, the Young Ireland League was formed.

On Sunday 27 May 1894, the Young Ireland League staged a commemoration of the Battle of Vinegar Hill. A procession with bands and banners made its way through Enniscorthy to Vinegar Hill where the assembly, estimated by the *Wexford Independent* to number 20,000 people, was addressed by Arthur Griffith. Other speakers followed and a letter of apology was read from Frederick J. Allen, a member of the Supreme Council of the IRB, who played a prominent part in the organisation of the '98 Centenary celebrations.

In 1897, the Young Ireland League held a series of meetings to appoint a City Hall committee to direct the centenary celebrations. Publicly the League expressed a wish to establish a broadly-based committee, but it was their intention to exclude constitutional politicians whether in the Redmond or Dillon wings of the divided Parliamentary Party. Nevertheless, Redmond had set out to cultivate extremist support by employing Frederick Allen as manager of his publishing company and also by recruiting former Fenians prisoners, to stand as Parnellite candidates for Parliament. This however did not give him easy access to membership of the Executive of the '98 Centenary Committee.

John Dillon, leader of the anti-Parnellites, resented the barring of elected public representatives from the centenary committee.[41] Although Redmond had failed to take over the City Hall movement, Dillon was suspicious of Redmond's influence with the IRB. John Dillon's ally, William O'Brien, warned that the commemorations could degenerate into a 'Redmondite faction' which would give 'Redmond the opportunity of posing in the only parts of the country where he has any strength'.[42]

Dillon determined to establish a centenary organisation of his own and, in response to his initiative, a United Irishmen's Centennial Association was formed in January 1898. In contrast to the City Hall committee, which sought to exclude members of Parliament and was said to exclude the clergy, this committee explicitly set out to include mayors, corporation members, Poor Law Board chairmen, clergymen and members of Parliament.[43]

VII

There were now two distinct national centenary organisations, in addition to a Wexford committee under Redmondite domination. The
national organisations professed a desire for harmony and unity, but in
their efforts to dominate the centenary the vituperation levelled at each
other threatened to do more harm than good. Despite the intention of
the City Hall committee to exclude politicians, the power of Redmondite
politics in Wexford inevitably meant that from the start the local organisation, succumbed to the weight of local political influence. It was
William O'Brien's intention 'to take the Wexford organisation out of the
wrong hands', but this was an impossible task. In Wexford, J.E.
Redmond, T.M. Healy, P. French, W. Redmond, and John Barry, the
former M.P. for Wexford, were included on an invitation list, but John
Dillon's name was conspicuously absent.

There was however, some ambiguity about Redmond's personal
family position; his paternal ancestor Walter Redmond had been a
yeoman in 1798, while his maternal ancestor William Kearney had been
an United Irishman.[44] There was a further ambiguity in the fact that John
Redmond, who had disavowed the methods of the republicans and was
well aware of the IRB involvement in the '98 centenary commemorations, was prepared to use the celebrations to further his own position.

The young
John Redmond

William Redmond M.P. addressed the crowd in the Market Square, Enniscorthy at
the unveiling of the dramatic bronze to Fr John Murphy and the young '98 pikeman
by the Franciscan historian, Fr Patrick Kavanagh on 31 May 1908. The Square was
the scene of bitter fighting on 28 May and 21 June 1798, and when William Redmond
attributed the measure of comparative freedom they enjoyed entirely to that bloody
struggle, there was a prolonged and enthusiastic response from the enormous crowd
which packed the Square and adjoining streets.

While the Government was prepared to turn a blind eye to the '98
celebrations, there was apprehension in the Orange Lodges. On 4 June,
the *Wexford Independent* published an address from the Grand Master
of the Orange Order in Belfast concerning the '98 commemoration celebration to be held in the city. It condemned the demonstration planned
for 6 June as:

> a flagitious display of sympathy with an armed insurrection
> which, above all things was characterised by a series of most foul
> and cowardly murders and massacres of innocent men and women
> whose only offence was their Protestantism.

Loyal men and women were asked to attend with double diligence to
their business on 6 June and reserve themselves for the 12 July celebrations which were expected to be of 'unusual interest and magnitude'.

Given the divisions within the Parliamentary Party, John Dillon,
leader of the anti-Parnellites, made the best use possible of the platform
presented by the '98 centenary celebrations to further his own political

aims. Invitations to speak on Centenary platforms were assiduously accepted. Urging William O'Brien to take up the New Ross invitation, Dillon wrote: 'it is of the utmost importance to get in touch with the people in that region. Not only is South Wexford to be considered but also South Kilkenny'.[45] Similarly, he instructed O'Brien to attend the Ballyellis ceremonies in a bid to offset Healyism. Dillon himself appeared on platforms from Belfast to Bodenstown and suffered exhaustion from the strain of his efforts.[46]

John Redmond, however, used the platform afforded to him as a Wexfordman during the '98 celebrations to advance his political status. Redmondite control in Wexford was secure and by 31 July dominated the centenary platforms there to the extent that the demonstration held at Three Rock Mountain in Wexford was a Parnellite meeting, composed mainly of Redmond followers.[47]

There were however, more fundamental divisions amongst Irish nationalists. At City Hall, John O'Leary presided over the weekly meetings of the '98 Centenary Executive Committee which planned the Dublin event; the erection of a Wolfe Tone monument on St Stephen's Green which was to be the highlight of the '98 celebrations.[48] The IRB had been the springboard of the '98 movement and its members worked tirelessly for the success of the Centenary celebrations. Their success was guaranteed by a settlement in May when a compromise was agreed with John Dillon's commemorative committee which provided for full representation of members of Parliament and clergy. At the St Stephen's Green celebration on 15 August, the City Hall Committee personalities continued to direct proceedings, but members of both factions within the Parliamentary Party were brought together on the same platform. The May compromise cleared the way for this broad spectrum of opinion and the speakers included John O'Leary, John Dillon, John Redmond, W.B. Yeats and William Rooney of the Gaelic League, who addressed the gathering in Irish.

VIII

Wexford was the main focus of the centenary celebrations and there Father P.F. Kavanagh played a central role. When the organising committee in Wexford had difficulty choosing a speaker to address their commemoration, the attendance left them in no doubt. There were cries of 'the priest'; 'Father Kavanagh' and 'it was the priests that led the Rebellion'. Father Kavanagh had done his work well, but now had to reconcile the involvement of the priests in the insurrection of '98 with the Church's condemnation Fenianism. 'Why did the rest of Ireland not rise in '98?' he asked. The answer was clear; 'it has always been so with secret societies. They promise much but when the hour comes to act they do little or nothing'.[49]

The occasion of the celebrations was an opportunity not to be missed and Kavanagh published a centenary edition of his history to mark the event. Again the Wexford conflict was isolated from events elsewhere and suggestions of a political conspiracy ignored. Once more, Father John Murphy initial involvement in outbreak is attributed to his sympathy for the plight of his people.[50]

This analysis stands in stark contrast to Luke Cullen's account of Murphy's address of 26 May:

> I know that they have me marked out. Look to the inhuman slaughter in Carnew, about nine miles from you and if the report of the butchery in Dunlavin be true, it is worse. Our jails are full of the best and the most beloved of our inhabitants and it may be our lot to be in company with them before to-morrow night.[51]

Such explicit references to arrested United Irish conspirators could not be accommodated within Kavanagh's model.

Kavanagh's interpretation of 1798 as a 'Fight for Faith and Fatherland' prevailed. Such analysis reflected his hopes for a separate and self-governed nation, the only form of government which would afford Catholics equality and freedom of conscience. These aspirations were in harmony with those of the IRB (some of whom he claimed as friends) and the militant Catholic Ancient Order of Hibernians of which he was Vice-President.

The IRB however, was a secret society and as such was anathema to the Church. Kavanagh attempted to balance this ambivalence by stressing the religious aspect of the insurrection in Wexford. While he appealed to Protestants to remember their patriots: from Molyneaux, Swift and Grattan through to Harvey, Grogan, Perry, Munro, McCracken, Tone, Lord Edward, Emmet and Parnell, the fact remained that ninety-nine per cent of those who died in '98 were Catholics Wexfordmen. Father Murphy was 'the lion hearted patriot, their skillful and daring leader'. Such analysis however, reflected the polarisation, the Catholic nationalism and narrowness of vision which was emerging in Ireland. Yet, there is in Kavanagh an apparent unawareness of the conflict between the varying emphases in what he said and wrote. Even his treatment of Father Murphy, 'the Great Souled Soggart', ignores the embarrassing conflict between him and Bishop James Caulfield.

It may be possible to cast Kavanagh as a forerunner of the politically radical priests of the age of the Gaelic League or later. His obsessive denouncement of secret societies however sets him apart. According to the *Wexford Independent*, Father Kavanagh had done 'more than any other man to perpetuate the spirit of the men of '98'.[52] On Vinegar Hill, in June 1898, he declared:

> we claim our rights as freemen to complete independence from foreign tyranny. God and our country alone can claim our allegiance. We abide our time.[53]

Time, however, ran out for Father Kavanagh in December 1918. On polling day, 18 December, in the 1918 General Elections, the eighty year old priest had visited the polling-booths on several occasions. That night he died in Wexford Friary. He was not to learn that out of 106 members returned for Irish constituencies 73 were Sinn Féin candidates, pledged to abstention from the English Parliament and to the claim of Irish independence.[54] He would have found it fitting that his last day on earth was spent assisting at the birth of what he would prefer to call a Catholic Nation.

A Chronology of 1798 in Wexford

Nicholas Furlong

1798	Winter and early spring; intensive United Irish planning in County Wexford.
12 March	Arrest of United Irish Leinster Directory at Oliver Bond's house, Dublin. Robert Graham, delegate of the Wexford United Irishmen avoids arrest by his late arrival.
30 March	Martial law proclaimed in Ireland; Privy Council declare Ireland to be in a state of rebellion.
16 April	Dr Caulfield and Ferns clergy meet in Enniscorthy to discuss crisis.
18 April	Declarations of loyalty from several Wexford parishes presented to Lord Lieutenant at Dublin Castle.
25 April	Twenty-seven magistrates assemble in Gorey agree to proclaim County Wexford. General Lake succeeds Abercromby as commander in chief in Ireland.
27 April	County Wexford proclaimed; North Cork Militia arrive in Wexford; severest measures imposed by magistrates, militia and yeomanry. Meeting of United Irish leadership in Lady Colclough's house, George's Street, Wexford – resumption of socialisation in Bagenal Harvey's home, Bargy Castle; 17 present, including four loyalists and diarist Sir Jonah Barrington (see *Personal Sketches*, p. 142-3). Present in either or both houses, Harvey, Cornelius Grogan, William Hatton, John Beauman, Matthew Keugh, John Colclough of Tintern, John Colclough of Ballyteigue Castle, John and Henry Shears and John Hay. United Irish revolutionary plans were freely discussed; Jonah Barrington was horrified and reported proceedings to Secretary Cooke at the Castle – this information and warning was not attended to.
17-18 May	Meeting of the new National Directory of United Irishmen.
23 May	Final warning to those possessing arms and offensive weapons to surrender same within fourteen days, issued by the High Sheriffs and magistrates of the county assembled as sessions, Wexford Court House. Anthony Perry of Inch arrested by North Cork Militia and broken down under 48 hours of torture at Gorey. He revealed the names of the United Irish leadership in County Wexford; these revelations were followed by the arrest of many United Irish leaders in Wexford.

157

24 May	Archibald Hamilton Jacob conducts the Enniscorthy Yeomen Cavalry to the village of Ballaghkeen where they flog a man to death. Thirty-five suspected United Irish prisoners shot in Dunlavin.
25 May	Twenty-four United Irish prisoners shot in the ball alley at Carnew. Four hundred and sixty United Irishmen killed in the unsuccessful attack on Carlow town.
26 May	The outbreak at the Harrow.
27 May	The Battle of Oulart.
28 May	The capture of Enniscorthy.
29 May	United Irish camp formed at the Three Rocks outside Wexford Town.
30 May	Battle of the Three Rocks and the taking of Wexford Town by the insurgents.
31 May	United Irish conference at Windmill Hill camp; United Irish forces divide into three; Establishment of civilian government in Wexford Town led by four Catholics and four Protestants.
1 June	Battle of Bunclody; engagement at Ballyminaun Hill.
4 June	Battle of Tubberneering and capture of Gorey by insurgents.
5 June	Battle of New Ross.
6 June	Rebellion breaks out in Ulster; Henry Joy McCracken issues proclamation calling Ulster United Irishmen to arms.
7 June	Capture and destruction of Carnew, County Wicklow.
9 June	United Irish defeat at the Battle of Arklow: United Irish retreat to Gorey.
13 June	United Irish defeat at the Battle of Ballinahinch, County Antrim.
16 June	Engagement of the Wexford and South Wicklow United Irishmen at Mountpleasant, near Tinahely, County Wicklow.
18 June	Engagement at Kilcavan Hill, near Carnew, County Wicklow.
20 June	Battle of Foulksmills; decisive battle in which the New Ross United Irish division challenged the crown forces under General Sir John Moore. Marquis Cornwallis sworn in as Lord Lieutenant.
21 June	Last battle for Enniscorthy and Vinegar Hill; recapture of Wexford Town by crown forces.

22 June	The famed 45-mile route march out of Wexford under Father John Murphy and Miles Byrne to Kiltealy, the Scullogue Gap and the engagement of Killedmond in County Carlow.
23 June	Engagement at Goresbridge, County Kilkenny.
24 June	Capture of Castlecomer, County Kilkenny.
25 June	United Irish camp at Keeffe's Hill, Slatt Lower, County Laois; receiving no local support, they turn back towards County Wexford.
26 June	Engagement at Kilcumney Hill, outside Goresbridge, County Carlow.
29 June	Battle of Ballyellis, near Monaseed, County Wexford; defeat of Ancient Britons.
2 July	Execution of Father John Murphy and his bodyguard, James Gallagher, at Tullow, County Carlow. Engagement at Ballygullen, Craanford, west of Gorey.
22 August	French force of 1,000 men under General Jean Humbert lands at Kilcumin, near Killala, County Mayo.
8 Sept.	General Humbert surrenders to Cornwallis at Ballinamuck, County Longford.

Notes

REINTERPRETING THE 1798 REBELLION IN COUNTY WEXFORD

1 Bartlett, *The Fall and Rise of the Irish Nation*; Keogh in this volume.
2 Burke, *Letter to a Noble Lord, Works*, p. 187.
3 Whelan, 'Politicisation in County Wexford'.
4 S. Cloney, 'South West Wexford in 1798' in *Jn. Wexford Historical Society*, xv (1994-95), pp 74-97.
5 Keogh, *French Disease*.
6 Caulfield-Troy Correspondence, Dublin Diocesan Archives.
7 Cited in Keogh, *French Disease*.
8 Cited Thomas Russell, *Journals and Memoirs* (ed.), C.J. Woods (Dublin, 1991).
9 Hay, *History of the Insurrection*.
10 Cloney, *A Personal Narrative*.
11 See Graham in this volume; Cullen, 'The internal politics of the United Irishmen'.
12 Graham, 'An union of power; the United Irish organisation'.
13 See Cullen in this volume.
14 Cullen, 'The 1798 rebellion in Wexford'.
15 Cullen, 'Politics and rebellion in Wicklow in the 1790s'.
16 Cullen, 'Burke, Ireland and Revolution'.
17 Furlong, *Father John Murphy of Boolavogue*.
18 Whelan, 'The role of the Catholic priest'.
19 Cited in Cullen, 'Politics and rebellion in Wicklow in the 1790s'.
20 Letter in the possession of John Devereux Kernan, New Haven, Connecticut, to whom I am grateful for permission to cite it.
21 See Graham in this volume.
22 See Gahan in this volume.
23 See Cleary in this volume.
24 Whelan, 'The Catholic community in eighteenth-century Wexford'.
25 See Bartlett in this volume.
26 Cited by Graham, 'An union of power'.
27 Whelan, 'Politicisation in County Wexford'.
28 *The Trial of William Byrne*.
29 Whelan, 'The Catholic community in eighteenth-century Wexford'.
30 Rev. Thomas Handcock, 'Narrative of 1798 in County Wexford', N.L.I., ms. 16,232.
31 Cited in T. Bartlett, 'The 1790s' in T. Bartlett and K. Jeffrey (eds), *A Military History of Ireland* (Cambridge, 1995).
32 Byrne, *Memoirs*, i, p. 155.
33 Bartlett in this volume.
34 Cited in Furlong, *Father John Murphy*.
35 Whelan, 'Catholics, politicisation and the 1798 rebellion'.
36 Cited in Furlong, *Father John Murphy*.
37 Cited in Whelan, *The Tree of Liberty*.
38 Ibid.
39 Gahan, *The People's Rising*.
40 Cullen, 'The 1798 rebellion in its eighteenth-century context'.

41 See Whelan, "'98 after '98: the politics of memory' in *The Tree of Liberty.*
42 Cited in Madden, *United Irishmen*, third series, i, p. 222.
43 See Kinsella in this volume.
44 Caulfield, *The Reply of the Rt. Rev. Dr Caulfield.*
45 Smyth, *The Men of No Property.*
46 Walter Walsh, 'Religion, ethnicity and history; clues to the cultural construction of law'.
47 See Bartlett in this volume.

SECTARIANISM AND 1798

 1 E.M. Johnston, *Ireland in the Eighteenth Century* (Dublin, 1974), p. 1.
 2 W. King, *The State of the Protestants of Ireland under the late King James' Government* (Dublin, 1691), p. 307.
 3 T. Bartlett, *The Fall and Rise of the Irish Nation: the Catholic Question 1690-1830* (Dublin, 1992); S.J. Connolly, *Religion Law and Power: The Making of Protestant Ireland 1660-1760* (Oxford, 1992)
 4 J. Kelly, ' "The Glorious and Immortal Memory": Commemoration and Protestant Identity in Ireland 1660-1800', *Proceedings of the Royal Irish Academy*, vol. 91, C. No. 2, p. 34.
 5 Bartlett, *Fall and Rise*, p. 49.
 6 H. Dundas to Westmorland, 26 December 1791 in A. Malcolmson, *John Foster; the politics of the Anglo-Irish Ascendancy* (Oxford, 1978), p. 415.
 7 Newenham, cited in R.B. McDowell, *Ireland in the Age of Imperialism and Revolution* (Oxford, 1979), p. 302.
 8 Peter Burrowes, cited in M. Elliott, *Wolfe Tone, prophet of Irish independence* (New Haven, 1989), p. 114.
 9 J. Coigley, *The Life of the Rev. James Coigley* (London, 1798), pp 12-13.
10 B. Clifford (ed.), *Scripture politics: selections from the writings of Rev. William Steel Dickson* (Belfast, 1991), p. 76.
11 D. Keogh, 'Maynooth: a Catholic seminary in a Protestant state', *History Ireland*, vol. 3, no. 3 (1995), pp 43-8.
12 Hussey to Edmund Burke, 27 Feb. 1795, T. Copeland (ed.), *The Correspondence of Edmund Burke*, vii, p. 162.
13 J. Smyth, 'The men of no popery: the origins of the Orange Order' in *History Ireland*, vol. 3, no. 3 (1995), pp 48-54.
14 Memoirs of James Hope cited in R.R. Madden, *The United Irishmen: their lives and times*, third series, vol. i (Dublin, 1846), pp 235-6.
15 Knox to Cooke, 13 August 1796, National Archives, Rebellion Papers, 620/24/106.
16 *F.D.J.*, 24 Sept. 1796.
17 J. Coigley in Keogh, *French Disease*, p. 101.
18 *F.D.J.*, 24 Sept. 1796.
19 E. Cooke to Wickham, 26 May 1798, H.O. 100/76/289-90.
20 Shannon to Boyle, 5 June 1798, P.R.O.N.I., D.2707/A3/3/76.
21 Shannon to Boyle, 12 June 1798, P.R.O.N.I, D.2707/A3/3/83.
22 W.E.H. Lecky, *A History of Ireland in the Eighteenth Century* (London, 1892), iv, 352.
23 Shannon to Boyle, 10 Sept. 1798, P.R.O.N.I, D.2707/A3/3/114.

24 For the most recent study of the rebellion in Wexford see D. Gahan, *The People's Rising: Wexford 1798* (Dublin, 1995).
25 G. Taylor, *A history of the rise, progress and suppression of the rebellion in the county of Wexford in the year 1798* (Dublin, 1800), p. 99.
26 D. Dickson, Foreword to Musgrave's *Memoirs of the Irish Rebellion of 1798* (Fourth edition, Wexford, 1995), p. i.
27 Veritas, *A vindication of the Roman Catholic clergy of the town of Wexford, during the late unhappy rebellion, from the groundless charges and illiberal insinuations of an anonymous writer, signed Verax* (Dublin, 1799).
28 Hussey to J.B. Clinch, Madden MSS, T.C.D., 873/197.
29 See T. Bartlett, *Fall and Rise*, pp 264-7.

THE UNITED IRISHMEN IN WEXFORD

1 P.F. Kavanagh, *The Wexford Rebellion* (Dublin, n.d. [1870?]).
2 W. Farrell (ed. R.J. McHugh), *Carlow in '98; the autobiography of William Farrell of Carlow* (Dublin, 1949); J. Holt, *Memoirs* (London, 1838).
3 T. Cloney, *A personal narrative of those transactions in the County of Wexford, in which the author was engaged, during the awful period of 1798* (Dublin, 1832).
4 The papers of Brother Luke Cullen are preserved in the Madden MSS, Trinity College Dublin and in the National Library of Ireland.
5 C. Dickson, *The life of Michael Dwyer, with some account of his companions* (Dublin, 1944).
6 E. Hay, *History of the Insurrection of the County of Wexford A.D. 1798* (Dublin, 1803).
7 M. Banim, *The Croppy Boy* (Dublin, 1828); C. Dickson, *The Wexford Rising of 1798* (Tralee, 1955).
8 R.R. Madden, *The United Irishmen, their lives and times*, revised edition, 4 vols. (London, 1857-60).
9 M. Byrne, *Memoirs* (Paris, 1863).
10 T. Bartlett, 'An end to moral economy; the Irish militia disturbances of 1793' in *Past and Present*, no. 99 (1983), pp 41-64 ; M. Elliott, *Partners in Revolution; the United Irishmen and France* (Yale, 1982).
11 W.E.H. Lecky, *A History of Ireland in the Eighteenth Century* (London, 1892), i, pp 45,93,99; iv, p. 345; C. Dickson, 1798 *Irish Sword*, ix (1969), pp 109-12.
12 L.M. Cullen, 'The Political Structure of the Defenders' in H. Gough and D. Dickson (eds), *Ireland and the French Revolution* (Dublin, 1990), pp 117-38.
13 T. Bartlett, 'Defenders and Defenderism in 1795' in *Irish Historical Studies*, xxiv (May 1985), pp 373-94; J. Brady, 'Lawerence O'Connor – A Meath Schoolmaster', *Irish Ecclesiastical Record*, (1937), pp 281-7.
14 See L.M. Cullen, 'Late eighteenth century politicisation in Ireland; problems in its study and its French links' in P. Bergeron and L.M. Cullen (eds), *Culture et pratiques politique en France et en Irlande XVIe-XVIIIe Siécle* (Paris, 1991), pp 137-58.
15 J. Stock, *A narrative of what passed at Killala … during the French invasion* (Dublin, 1800); J. Gordon, *History of the Rebellion in Ireland* (London, 1803).
16 Diary of Revd James Little, in *Analecta Hibernica*, vol. II.
17 L.M. Cullen, 'The internal politics of the United Irishmen' in D. Dickson, D. Keogh and K. Whelan (eds), *The United Irishmen* (Dublin, 1993), pp 176-96.

DUBLIN IN 1798

1 Plan for 'National Guard' (Reb. Papers, 620/54/15).
2 W.J. MacNeven, *Pieces of Irish history illustrative of the condition of the Catholics of Ireland and of the origins and progress of the political system of the United Irishmen and of their transactions with the Anglo-Irish government* (New York, 1807), p. 204.
3 Mac Neven, *Pieces*, p. 195.
4 Camden to Portland, 6 Aug. 1796 (PRO[L.], HO/100/62/153-163).
5 *Report of the Committee of Secrecy of House of Commons and the House of Lords of Ireland* (Dublin, 1798). Sec., app. dccclxxxi.
6 McNally to Cooke, 14 May 1797; E. Boyle to Sirr, 12 May 1797 (Reb. Papers, 620/10/121/56; 620/30/61).
7 Information of McGuckin, Aug. 1798 (Reb. Papers, 620/3/32/13).
8 Memoire, p.12 (Reb. Papers 620/44/1).
9 Rep. Comm. Sec., app. dccclxxi; information of James McGuckin, Aug. 1798 (Reb. Papers, 620/3/32/13).
10 Higgins to Cooke, 3 May 1797 (Reb. Papers 620/18/14).
11 Camden to Portland (enclosure, 19 April 1798), 25 April 1798 (PRO[L], HO/100/76/138-139).
12 Rep. Comm. Sec., app. dccclxxi.
13 Camden to Portland (enclosure re Reynolds' information), 11 Mar. 1798 (PRO[L], HO/100/75/207-208).
14 Information of McGuckin, Aug. 1798 (Reb. Papers, 620/3/32/13).
15 Camden to Portland (enclosure re Reynolds' information), 11 Mar. 1798 (PRO[L], HO/100/75/207-208).
16 Memoire, p.13 (Reb. Papers 620/44/1).
17 Camden to Portland (enclosure from McNally, 25 Feb. 1798), 26 Feb. 1798 (PRO[L], HO/100/75/128-135).
18 Thomas Boyle to Cooke, 20 Feb. and Mar. 1798 (Reb. Papers, 620/18/3).
19 Pakenham, *Year of Liberty*, p. 119.
20 Sirr Papers (TCD MS 869, 9/84,85).
21 Sproule to Lees, 14 May 1798 (Reb. Papers, 620/51/40).
22 Memoire, p.13 (Reb. Papers 620/44/1).
23 Rep. Comm. Sec., app. dccccxxviii.
24 Annesley to Cooke, 21 Mar. 1798 (Reb. Papers, 620/36/40).
25 Anon., 17 May 1798 (Reb. Papers, 620/37/97).
26 Higgins to Cooke, 20 May 1798 (Reb. Papers, 620/18/14).
27 Information of McConkey 6 June 1798; anon., 25 June 1798; information of Blackham, 25 June 1798 (Reb. Papers, 620/38/67; 620/38/232; 620/38/234).
28 Camden to Portland, 11 May 1798 (PRO[L], HO/100/76/170-177).
29 Camden to Portland, 26 May 1798 (PRO[L], HO/100/76/291-292).
30 Sproule to Lees, 21 May 1798 (Reb. Papers, 620/51/21).
31 Sproule to Lees, undated ['Wednesday morning, camp'](Reb. Papers, 620/51/30).
32 Camden to Portland, 20 May 1798 (PRO[L], HO/100/76/220-221); Sproule to Lees, 15 May 1798 (Reb. Papers, 620/51/39).
33 Sproule to Lees, 16 May 1798 (Reb. Papers, 620/51/31).
34 Sproule to Lees, 23 May 1798 (Reb. Papers, 620/51/18).
35 Sproule to Lees, 23 May 1798 (Reb. Papers, 620/51/25).
36 Musgrave, *Rebellions*, p. 214; Higgins to Cooke, 25 May (Reb. Papers, 620/18/14).

37 Worthington to —, 24 Aug. 1802 (Reb. Papers, 620/10/125/4).
38 Sunset on 23 May was at 8.30 p.m., GMT, and darkness, depending on weather conditions, up to an hour later. According to contemporary accounts the weather was fine in Dublin in May 1798 which would place dusk at about 9.30 p.m., GMT. But until 1916 'Dublin Mean Time' applied to Ireland which was twenty-five minutes behind GMT which would place dusk in Dublin on 23 May 1798 at 9.05 p.m., local time. If the Yeomanry assembled at about 9 p.m. in anticipation of a rising at 10 p.m. it bears out Musgrave's claim that 'the rebel drums were to have beaten to arms an hour after ours'.
39 Barrington, *The rise and fall of the Irish nation*, pp 214-15.
40 Musgrave, *Rebellions*, p. 213.
41 G. Ó Tuathaigh, *Ireland before the Famine, 1798-1848*, p. 19.
42 Sproule to Lees, 21 May 1798 (Reb. Papers, 620/51/21).
43 Sheares' letter to Neilson, Rep. Comm. Sec., app. dccccix.
44 Musgrave, *Rebellions*, p. 215.
45 Musgrave, *Rebellions*, pp 211-13.
46 NL MS 637, p. 210.
47 Musgrave, *Rebellions*, pp 210-15; *F. Jnl*, 26 May 1798.
48 NL MS 637, p. 435.
49 Pakenham, *Year of Liberty*, p. 124.
50 Musgrave, *Rebellions*, p. 217.
51 Musgrave, *Rebellions*, pp 212-13.
52 Musgrave, *Rebellions*, pp 212-27; *F. Jnl*, 24-26 May 1798; *FDJ*, 26 May 1798; Camden to Portland, 25 May 1798 (PRO[L], HO/100/76/274-276).
53 Author?, *Fingal in '98*, p. 186; Musgrave, *Rebellions*, p. 225.
54 Daniel Gahan, 'The Military Strategy of the Wexford United Irishmen in 1798' in *History Ireland*, vol. 1, no. 4 (1993), pp 28-32.

THE BATTLE OF OULART HILL

1 N. Furlong, *Father John Murphy of Boolavogue, 1753-1798*, p. 58.
2 Cahill's 1817 Bruen Estate Map Book, County Museum, Enniscorthy Castle; Peter Foley's memoir in Luke Cullen papers which are contained in the Madden MSS, TCD.
3 Luke Cullen, MSS, TCD.
4 T. Cloney, *Narrative* also mentions the Dorans, p. 14.
5 An tAthair Séamas S. de Vál, *Oulart in '98*, p. 8. A private publication.
6 Peter Foley in Luke Cullen MSS, TCD.
7 Edward Hay, *History*, pp 86-7.
8 Richard Musgrave, *Memoirs of the Different Rebellions in Ireland from the arrival of the English...*', p. 328.
9 Peter Foley, in Cullen MSS.
10 Wheeler and Broadley, *The War in Wexford*, p. 86, quoting of the Camolin Cavalry Day-Book.
11 Brian Cleary, 'The Battle of Oulart Hill', *The Past* (1995).
12 Hay, *History*, p. 89.
13 Peter Foley in Cullen MSS.
14 Peter Foley in Cullen MSS.
15 Patrick Kavanagh, *A Popular History of the Insurrection of 1798*.

16 Peter Foley in Cullen MSS.
17 Cahill's Map from 1817.
18 Cloney, *Narrative*, p. 11.
19 Kavanagh, *Popular History*, p. 104.
20 Henry McAnally, *The Irish Militia, 1793-1806*, p. 48.
21 Ainsworth, A.J. Report on Private Collections re the Lombard Papers, N.L.I.
22 Hay, *History*, p. 82.
23 Ibid., p. 82.
24 Musgrave, *Rebellions*, p. 341.
25 Peter Foley in Cullen MSS.
26 Furlong, *Father Murphy*, p. 58; Wheeler and Broadly, *The War in Wexford*, pp 90-2.
27 Peter Foley in Cullen MSS.
28 Cloney, *Narrative*, p. 11
29 Peter Foley in Cullen MSS.
30 Ibid.
31 Ibid.
32 Ibid.
33 Ibid.
34 See note on the Hyland Pike in *The Past* (1995), p. 95.

THE MILITARY PLANNING OF THE 1798 REBELLION IN WEXFORD

1 Typical of these are: Sir Richard Musgrave, *Memoirs of the different rebellions in Ireland* (Dublin, 1801); George Taylor, *A history of the rise, progress and suppression of the rebellion in the county of Wexford* (Dublin, 1800); W.H. Maxwell, *History of the Irish Rebellion in 1798* (London, 1845); Thomas Pakenham, *The Year of Liberty, the Great Irish Rebellion of 1798* (London, 1969).
2 See Thomas Cloney, *A personal narrative of those transactions in the county of Wexford, in which the author was engaged, during the awful period of 1798* (Dublin 1932); Edward Hay, *History of the insurrection of the county of Wexford, AD 1798* (Dublin, 1803); Rev. Patrick Kavanagh, *A popular history of the insurrection of 1798* (Dublin, 1870).
3 L.M. Cullen, 'The 1798 Rebellion in County Wexford: United Irishman organisation, membership and leadership', in Kevin Whelan (ed.) *Wexford: History and Society* (Dublin 1987), pp 248-95.
4 Nancy Curtin, 'The United Irish Organisation in Ulster, 1795-1798' in David Dickson *et al.*, *The United Irishmen: republicanism, radicalism and rebellion* (Dublin, 1993), pp 209-21; and her *The United Irishmen: Popular Politics in Ulster and Dublin, 1791-1798* (Oxford, 1994); Thomas Graham, ' "An union of power"? The United Irish organisation' in David Dickson *et al.*, *The United Irishmen*, pp 244-55.
5 Graham, 'An union of power', pp 254-5.
6 Cullen, 'United Irishmen organisation', p. 267.
7 Dickson, *Wexford*, pp 200-13
8 Cullen, 'United Irishman organisation', p. 290
9 James Alexander, *Some account —— of the rebellion in the County of Wexford* (Dublin, 1800), p. 25.

10 Miles Byrne, *Memoirs*, i (Dublin, 1906), pp 25-6.
11 Cullen, 'United Irishman Organisation' p 28; Nicholas Furlong, *Father John Murphy of Boolavogue, 1753-1798* (Dublin, 1991), pp 23, 43-4; Charles Dickson *The Wexford Rising in 1798: Its Causes and Course* (Tralee, 1955), pp 43-7.
12 Kyan was a prisoner as late as 4 June; see Byrne, *Memoirs*, i, p. 76.
13 Byrne, *Memoirs*, pp 30-1.
14 See D. Gahan, 'The Military Strategy of the Wexford United Irishmen in 1798', *History Ireland* vol. 1 no. 4 (1993), pp 29-30.
15 Cloney, *Personal Narrative*, pp 14-15; for a modern assessment of Cloney's account see Cullen 'United Irishmen organisation', pp 255-6.
16 NLI Ms 11,994 'Kalender compiled for the Year 1798 by John Watson Stewart' (Dublin 1798).
17 Although coloured by his biased view, Musgrave's account of these early raids is probably reliable in its general outlines; see *Rebellions*, i, pp 404-11.
18 James Gordon, *History of the Rebellion in Ireland in the Year 1798* (London, 1801), pp 89-90; For a meticulously detailed description of this movement see Cullen, 'United Irishman organisation', pp 289-92.
19 Gordon, *Rebellion*, pp 89-90; Luke Cullen, *Personal Recollections of Wexford and Wicklow Insurgents of 1798* (Enniscorthy, 1959), pp 16-17
20 Dickson (*Wexford Rising*, pp 68-9) notes that roads leading off in four different directions joined at its summit.
21 Byrne, *Memoirs*, i, pp 42-51; William Snowe, *A fair and candid statement of transactions at Enniscorthy on the 28th of May and at Wexford on the 30th of May, 1798* (Dublin, 1801), 1-14.
22 Byrne, *Memoirs*, i, pp pp 47-50.
23 Ibid., pp 52-9; Hay, *Insurrection*, pp 95-112.
24 Byrne, *Memoirs*, i, pp 56-7.
25 We get a sense of the state of the town's defences in Alexander, *Account*, pp 27-31.
26 For an excellent description of this gathering see Furlong, *Father Murphy*, pp 87-9.
27 Byrne, *Memoirs*, i, p. 63; Furlong, *Murphy*, pp 89-90.
28 Hay, *Insurrection*, pp 125-6.
29 Ibid., p. 141.
30 They spent part of this time drilling, in preparation for upcoming battles; see Byrne, *Memoirs*, i, pp 68-9.
31 Dickson, *Wexford Rising*, pp 107-34.
32 See Furlong, *Father Murphy*, pp 113-14 and Cloney *Personal Narrative*, p. 37; Dickson *Wexford*, p. 111.
33 Byrne, *Memoirs*, i, pp 109-23; Hay, *Insurrection*, pp 159-64.
34 Miles Byrne makes no effort to hide his frustration at this difference of opinion, *Memoirs*, i, p. 121.
35 Hay, *Insurrection*, pp 194-5.
36 Miles Byrne, *Memoirs*, i, pp 120-1.
37 Roche's behaviour is puzzling, see Cullen, *Recollections*, p. 35; Dickson, *Wexford*, p. 163.
38 Miles Byrne, *Memoirs*, i, pp 151-2.
39 Cullen, *Recollections*, p. 42.
40 Hay, *Insurrection*, pp 251-3.
41 Furlong, *Father Murphy*, pp 136-56; Cullen, *Recollections*, pp 42-50.

42 Byrne, *Memoirs*, i, pp 173-4.
43 Cullen, *Recollections*, pp 53-60.
44 Ibid., p. 69.

LOCAL OR COSMOPOLITAN?: THE STRATEGIC IMPORTANCE OF
WEXFORD IN 1798

1 Charles Vallency, *The Defences of Southern Ireland* (1797), Ferns Diocesan
   Archives; manuscript copy, pages not numbered, p. 17.
2 Nicholas Furlong, 'Life in Wexford Port 1600-1800', in K. Whelan and W. Nolan
   (eds), *Wexford; History and Society* (Dublin, 1987), pp 151-8.
3 Furlong, 'Life in Wexford Port 1600-1800'.
4 Jane H. Ohlmeyer, 'The Dunkirk of Ireland; Wexford Privateers during the
   1640s', in *Journal of the Wexford Historical Society* (1988-9), pp 23-49.
5 Fergal Grannell, *The Franciscans in Wexford* (Wexford, 1975), pp 17-29.
6 Peadar J. Sinnott, 'Duncannon Fort', *Journal Old Wexford Society*, iii (1970), p.
   79.
7 Charles Vallency, Defences, p. 11.
8 Charles Vallency, Defences, p. 14.
9 R. Roche and O. Merne, *Saltees* (Wexford, 1977), p. 59.
10 Miles Byrne, *Memoirs*, i (Paris, 1863), pp 66-7; Charles Dickson, *The Wexford
   Rising in 1798* (Tralee, 1955).
11 Thomas Cloney, *Narrative*, pp 29-30: Miles Byrne, *Memoirs*, i, p. 81; Edward
   Hay, *History*, p. 121.

MILES BYRNE: UNITED IRISHMAN, IRISH EXILE AND 'BEAU SABREUR'

1 Stephen Gwynn (ed.), *Memoirs of Miles Byrne, edited by his widow* (Dublin,
   1907), p. iii.
2 Fanny Horner, sister of Francis Horner, *Edinburgh Review* writer and author of
   a well-regarded treatise on the linen industry. Fanny Horner was self-effacing:
   she never gives her name and refers to herself as Miles Byrne's widow. They married some time after Byrne retired from the French army, and there were no children. See W.J. Fitzpatrick, *The Sham Squire and the Informers of 1798, with jot-
   tings about Ireland seventy years ago* (6th edn., Dublin, 1862), p. 189. My thanks
   to Fr Lorry Kehoe, and to Mr Michael Lyons for information on Miles Byrne's
   wife.
3 *Memoirs of Miles Byrne edited by his widow* (1st edition, 3 volumes, Paris, 1863;
   facsimile reprint edition, three volumes, retaining separate pagination, bound as
   one, Shannon, 1972). All references to Byrne's *Memoirs* are to the facsimile edition.
4 All previous accounts of the rebellion in Wexford are now superseded by Daniel
   Gahan, *The People's Rising: the 1798 rebellion in Wexford* (Dublin, 1995).
5 For the careers of Holt and Dwyer see Thomas Bartlett, 'Masters of the
   Mountains: the insurgent careers of Joseph Holt and Michael Dwyer' in Kenneth
   Hannigan (ed.), *Wicklow; History and Society* (Dublin 1994), pp 379-410.
6 Byrne, *Memoirs*, iii, p. 11.
7 Robert Emmet is long overdue a modern study, but pending that, see Marianne

Elliott, *Partners in Revolution: the United Irishmen and France* (New Haven, 1982), pp 282-322.

8 I have drawn extensively on Byrne's service dossier no. 49,404, in the French military archives at Vincennes, Paris.

9 See for examples, Chas. Ross (ed.), *Cornwallis Correspondence* (3 vols., London, 1859); Sir J.F. Maurice (ed.), *The Diary of Sir John Moore* (2 vols., London, 1904); Lord Dunfermline (ed.), *Lieutenant General Sir Ralph Abercromby* (Edinburgh, 1861); I.H. Mackay Scobie, *An Old Highland Fencible Corps, an account of the Reay Fencible Regiment of Foot ... with an account of its services in Ireland during the rebellion of 1798* (Edinburgh, 1914); Nuala Costello (ed), 'Jobit Narrative', *Analecta Hibernica*, no. 11 (1941); General Sarrazin, 'An officer's account of the French campaign in Ireland', *Irish Sword*, ii, (1955), pp 110-18, 161-71).

10 Edward Hay, *History of the Insurrection of the county of Wexford, A.D. 1798* (Dublin, 1803).

11 W.T. Tone (ed.), *Life of Theobald Wolfe Tone* (2 vols., Washington D.C. 1826).

12 W.J. MacNeven, *Pieces of Irish History* (New York, 1807); C.H. Teeling, *Personal Narrative of the Irish Rebellion of 1798* (Belfast, 1832; W.H. Drummond (ed.), *The Autobiography of Archibald Hamilton Rowan* (reprint edition, Shannon, 1972).

13 Thomas Cloney, *Personal Narrative* (Dublin, 1832); Roger McHugh (ed.) *Carlow in '98; the autobiography of William Farrell of Carlow* (Dublin, 1948).

14 For a general account of the military history of the 1790s, including the rebellion, see Thomas Bartlett, 'Defence, Counter-insurgency and Rebellion: Ireland in the 1790s' in T. Bartlett and K. Jeffery (ed.), *A Military History of Ireland* (Cambridge, 1996), pp 247-93.

15 Byrne, *Memoirs*, i, pp 67-8, 165.

16 Ibid., p. 285.

17 Ibid., pp 81-2.

18 Ibid., pp 66-7, 69, 174.

19 Ibid., pp 138, 94-5, 180.

20 Ibid., p. 285.

21 Ibid., p. 132.

22 Ibid., pp 178.

23 Ibid., pp 123, 132.

24 Ibid., p. 162.

25 Ibid., i, p. 179.

26 Ibid., p. 186.

27 Ibid., p. 173.

28 Ibid., p. 155.

29 Ibid., pp 275-6.

30 Edward Hay, *History of the Insurrection of the County of Wexford. A.D. 1798* (Dublin, 1803): For modern assessments of the role of the Catholic priest in the Wexford rebellion see Kevin Whelan, 'The role of the Catholic priest in the 1798 rebellion in county Wexford' in Kevin Whelan (ed), *Wexford, History and Society* (Dublin, 1987), pp 296-315; see also Dáire Keogh, *'The French Disease': The Catholic Church and Radicalism 1790-1800* (Dublin, 1993).

31 R.R. Madden, *The United Irishmen, their lives and times* (7 volumes, London, 1842-5).

32 See especially, Sir Richard Musgrave, *Memoirs of the Different Rebellions in Ireland ...* (Dublin, 1802; rept. ed., Fort Wayne, Indiana, 1995).

33 Byrne, *Memoirs*, i, p. 67.

34 Ibid., ii, pp 124
35 For a short discussion of insurgency and counter-insurgency in Spain, see Charles Esdaile, 'The British army and the guerilla war in Spain' in Alan J. Guy (ed.), *The Road to Waterloo: The British Army and the Struggle against Revolutionary and Napoleonic France, 1793-1815* (London, 1990), pp 132-41.
36 Byrne, *Memoirs*, ii, p. 83.
37 Ibid., p. 80.
38 Byrne, *Memoirs*, ii, pp 91-3.
39 Byrne's adjective for his counter-insurgency duty: Byrne, *Memoirs*, ii, p. 79.
40 Byrne to Marquis de Lauriston, 19 June 1823: Byrne dossier, Vincennes; Byrne, *Memoirs*, iii, p. 85.
41 Byrne, *Memoirs*, i, p.167; see documents concerning events on Vinegar Hill published in Musgrave, *Memoirs of the Irish Rebellion of 1798* (Dublin, 1802, rept. ed., Fort Wayne, Indiana, 1995), appendix xix, pp. 761-8.
42 Byrne dossier, Vincennes: presumably the date is that on which he was sworn into the United Irishmen. He concluded his service in the rebellion precisely on 15 November 1798, when he arrived in Dublin and went into hiding.
43 Byrne dossier, Vincennes: 'The exponent, born on the 20 March 1780 joined the service of France on 10 January on the outbreak of the insurrection [which was] evidently instigated, directed and commanded by French agents and generals. He took part during the years 1797 and 1798 in that war to which France attached so much value and which became the source of such great sacrifices. The fate of the armies, however, not having been favourable in this respect, the unfortunate Irish who had responded to the appeal of the French government left Ireland and came to France where they were welcomed as brothers.'
44 Byrne was very close to MacNeven in 1803, and he refers to him collecting narratives of '98 with a view to publication. Byrne, *Memoirs*, iii, pp 26, 65.
45 A recent history of the Irish Legion is J. Gallaher, *Napoleon's Irish Legion* (Carbondale, iii, 1993); see also P. Carles, 'Le Corps Irlandais au service de la France sous le Consulat et l'Empire', *Revue Historique des Armées*, 2, 1976, pp 25-54; Marianne Elliott, *Partners in Revolution: the United Irishmen and France* (New Haven, 1982), pp 330-40.
46 Byrne, *Memoirs*, iii, p. 69.
47 Ibid., pp. 53-4, 67, 84n-85n.
48 Ibid., ii, pp 82-3.
49 Ibid., ii, p. 82.
50 Ibid., ii, pp 215-16.
51 Ibid., ii, p. 75.
52 Ibid., pp 106, 124.
53 Byrne to Duc de Bellune, 30 Sept. 1815: Byrne dossier, Vincennes.
54 '... a deceitful, wicked and very dangerous man; has been a furious partisan of Bonaparte and will never change. Should be closely watched wherever he lives': Report to the Minister of War, 4 March 1817; Comment by Comte Maurice de Caraman, n.d. [c. 1817]: Byrne dossier, Vincennes.
55 '... He appears to be of sober habits and peaceful conduct. The only people he sees are a guard ... an officer of the Garde Royale and two Professors of the Irish College. These last two are his countrymen. Generally he spends his evenings at the shows or at the comic opera': Police report on Byrne, February 1817: Byrne dossier, Vincennes.
56 For Clarke, see Marianne Elliott, *Wolfe Tone, Prophet of Irish Independence* (New Haven, 1989), pp 293-7.

57 Byrne, *Memoirs*, iii, pp 85, 117.
58 Byrne dossier, Vincennes; Byrne, *Memoirs*, ii, p. 21.
59 Byrne, *Memoirs*, iii, pp 119-20.
60 Byrne dossier, Vincennes; Byrne, *Memoirs*, ii, p. 152.
61 Byrne, *Memoirs*, ii, p. 152
62 Ibid., iii, pp 8, 24-8. Typically Byrne shrugged off the hardship of the early years in Paris, 'I having known the starvation suffered in the mountains of the county of Wicklow': *Memoirs.*, iii, p. 8.
63 Ibid., p. 21.
64 Ibid., pp 84, 158, 195.
65 Ibid., pp 290-1.
66 Ibid., ii, p. 145 (*Gil Blas*); iii, p. 283 (Rousseau), pp 281-2 (*Captain Rock*), p. 48 (Campbell); Byrne dossier, Vincennes, (knowledge of Spanish), p. 329 (ruins).
67 Byrne, *Memoirs*, iii, pp 134-5, 238.
68 Ibid., p. 203.
69 Ibid., pp 87-8, 92-3.
70 Ibid., p. 304.
71 Ibid.i, p. 282.
72 Ibid., p. 301.
73 Ibid., pp 296, 285-7, 104.
74 Ibid., p. 145.
75 Ibid., pp 312-13.
76 There is an intriguing letter among the Rebellion Papers in the National Archives, Dublin concerning Miles Byrne. The letter is anonymous and undated, but after 1803, and states baldly that 'Miles Byrne, stepbrother to Edward Kennedy ... has arrived in this country, and that he is at present among his friends in Wexford, that he appears as a French officer. This Byrne was one of the most active men connected with Emmet in the affair of 1803.' The writer continues, 'I don't think, Sir, this government was sufficiently acquainted with Byrne's character or they would not suffer him to come into this country' (Rebellion Papers, 620/13/178/45). There is no corroborating evidence for this claim and, though the detail is compelling, it is surely impossible that Byrne would have failed to mention such a trip.
77 Byrne, *Memoirs*, iii, pp 299-300.
78 Ibid., p. 307.
79 Ibid., pp 304-5.
80 Byrne dossier, Vincennes; Byrne, *Memoirs*, iii, pp 314-15. Byrne appears to have received the award of Chevalier de St Louis sometime later. The award is listed on his gravestone in Montmartre.
81 Byrne, *Memoirs*, ii, p. 152; ibid., iii, p. 45.
82 Ibid., iii, p. 307: Halliday also gave Byrne money to get married in 1835.
83 Ibid., p. 317
84 Ibid., p. 327; ibid., ii, p. 75.
85 Fanny Byrne claimed that Byrne had planned a detailed account of his campaign in Greece: Byrne, *Memoirs*, iii, p. 334.
86 Byrne, *Memoirs*, i, pp 197-9.
87 Report on Byrne by General Chabert, 4 Sept. 1830: Byrne dossier, Vincennes.
88 Byrne, *Memoirs*, iii, p. 336.
89 Ibid., p. 237.
90 Gustave de Beaumont, *Irlande, sociale, politicale, religieuse* (Paris, 1840); Byrne, *Memoirs*, iii, pp 253-4.

91 Byrne, *Memoirs*, iii, p. 228.
92 O'Neill to Byrne, 1837, Byrne, *Memoirs*, ii, pp i-ii.
93 Byrne to W.J. Fitzpatrick, 18 Feb. 1854 in Chas. Dickson, *The Wexford Rising in 1798* (Tralee, 1955), p. 219.
94 Byrne to W.J. Fitzpatrick, 18 Feb. 1854 in Chas. Dickson, *The Wexford Rising in 1798* (Tralee, 1955), p. 219.

1798 CLAIMED FOR CATHOLICS: FATHER KAVANAGH, FENIANS
AND THE CENTENARY CELEBRATIONS

1 Kavanagh, *The Wexford Rebellion*, advertisement for second ed. included in 3rd ed. p. vii.
2 Denis Mack Smyth, *The making of Italy 1796-1870* (New York, 1968), p. 41; P.F. Kavanagh, 'Two Famous Irish Patriots' in *Catholic Bulletin* (1913) vol. iii, p. 340.
3 L. O'Broin, 'Revolutionary nationalism in Ireland, the I.RB 1858-1924': see p. 108 in T.W. Moody (ed.), *Nationality and the pursuit of national independence* (Belfast, 1978)
4 F.S.L. Lyons, *John Dillon – a biography* (London, 1968) p. 15.
5 P.F. Kavanagh, Lecture; Full text pub. in *Wexford People*, 15 Jan. 1898.
6 P.F. Kavanagh, *The Wexford Rebellion*, 1st ed. (Dublin, publication undated [*c*.1870?]) p. 17.
7 P.F. Kavanagh, *The history of the insurrection of '98*, centenary ed. (Cork, 1898) p. 84.
8 P.F. Kavanagh, *The Wexford Rebellion*, 1st ed., p. 118.
9 P.F. Kavanagh, *A popular history of the insurrection of 1798* (Dublin 1874). p. 94.
10 P.J. Corish (ed.), *History of Irish Catholicism*, v (Dublin, 1967), p. 16.
11 Ibid., p. 41.
12 Ibid., p. 47
13 P.F. Kavanagh, *A popular history*, centenary ed. (Cork, 1898), p. 92.
14 P.J. Corish (ed.), *History of Irish Catholicism*, iv, *Freeman's Journal* 15, 16, 26 Sept. 3, 23, 31 Oct., 11 Nov. 1873.
15 *The People* (Wexford), 15 January 1898.
16 Miles, *Memoirs*, i, pp 7-10.
17 Kavanagh, centenary ed. p. 225.
18 Byrne, *Memoirs*, i, p. 9.
19 Kavanagh, cent. ed., p. 84.
20 Ibid., p. 92.
21 Ibid., p. 95.
22 John Turpin, 'Oliver Sheppard's 1798 memorials' in *Irish Arts Review* 1990-91, p. 78.
23 Kavanagh, note C on Chap. 3, 1st ed., p. 116.
24 Byrne, *Memoirs*, i, p. 53.
25 Kavanagh, centenary ed., p. 103.
26 Kevin Whelan, 'The role of the Catholic priests in the 1798 Rebellion in County Wexford' in K. Whelan and W. Nolan (eds), *Wexford History and Society* (Dublin, 1987), p. 296.
27 Kavanagh, centenary ed., pp 113-15, 148.
28 Lyons, *John Dillon*, p. 16.
29 Kavanagh, 'Two famous Irish patriots ' in *Catholic Bulletin* vol. 3 (1913), p. 340.

30 Ibid.
31 National Archives, C.S.O.R.P 1877/8058.
32 *Wexford Independent,* October 1878.
33 National Archives, C.S.O.R.P. 1877/8058, *Wexford Independent,* 2 October 1878.
34 Emmett Larkin, *The Roman Catholic Church and the creation of the modern Irish State 1878–1896* (Dublin 1975), pp 34-5.
35 Kavanagh, centenary edition, p.vii; *The People,* 15 January 1898.
36 *The People*, 15 January 1898; see also Kavanagh, cent. ed., pp vii, 294.
37 Kavanagh, *Patriotism,* p. 33.
38 Ibid., p. 31.
39 L. O'Broin, 'Revolutionary nationalism in Ireland' in Moody (ed.), *Nationality and the pursuit of national independence,* p. 992; see also National Archives, C.B.S.13419/s.
40 T.J. O'Keefe, 'The 1898 efforts to celebrate the United Irishmen; the '98 centennial' in *Eire-Ireland,* xxiii 2 (Summer 1988), pp 51-73 citing *Irish Independent,* 23 June 1897; see also McBride White, Anna and Jeffares, A. Norman, *The Gonne Yeats Letters,* p. 468, n. 3.
41 Minute book of Oliver Bond '98 Club MSS 3730.
42 O'Brien William papers, MSS 8555/14/15 N.L.I.
43 *Freeman's Journal,* 15 and 18 March, 1898.
44 *The People,* 1 and 4 June, 1898.
45 Wm. O'Brien. MSS 8555/14/15, N.L.I.
46 Ibid.
47 K. Whelan, *Wexford History and Society,* p. 485.
48 Marcus Bourke, *John O'Leary, a study in Irish separatism* (Tralee 1967), p. 218.
49 Kavanagh lecture, *The People,* 15 January 1898.
50 Kavanagh, cent. ed., p. 95.
51 Cullen Luke, *Personal Recollections of Wicklow and Wexford Insurgents of 1798* (Enniscorthy 1959), p. 9.
52 *Wexford Independent,* 2 November 1898.
53 *The People,* 12 October 1898.
54 Henry Robert Mitchell, *The evolution of Sinn Féin* (Dublin, 1937), p. 27.

Select Bibliography

Bartlett, Thomas, 'An end to Moral Economy: The Irish Militia disturbances of 1793' in *Past & Present*, lxc (1983), pp 41-64.

——, *The Fall and Rise of the Irish Nation: The Catholic Question 1690-1830* (Dublin, 1992).

——, 'Nationalism in Eighteenth-Century Ireland' in O'Dea and Whelan (eds.), *Nations and Nationalisms*, pp 79-88.

Burke, Edmund, *The Works of the Rt. Hon. Edmund Burke*, 2 vols. (London, 1834).

——, *The Writings and Speeches of Edmund Burke*, vol. iii; *The French Revolution*, (ed.) L.G. Mitchell (Oxford, 1989).

Byrne, Miles, *Memoirs of Miles Byrne, Chef de Bataillon in the Service of France*, edited by his widow (2 vols., Paris, 1863).

The Tryal of William Byrne of Ballymanus (Dublin, 1799).

Caulfield, James, *The Reply of the Rt. Revd Dr Caulfield, Roman Catholic Bishop and the R.C. Clergy of Wexford to the Misrepresentations of Sir Richard Musgrave, Bart* (Dublin, 1801).

Cloney, Thomas, *A Personal Narrative of those Transactions in the County of Wexford in which the author was engaged at the awful period of 1798* (Dublin, 1832).

Colley, Linda, *Britons: Forging the Nation 1707-1837* (New Haven, 1992).

——, 'Britishness and Otherness: An Argument' in O'Dea and Whelan (eds.), *Nations and Nationalisms*, pp 61-77.

Cullen, L.M., *The Emergence of Modern Ireland 1600-1900* (London, 1981).

——, 'The 1798 Rebellion in its Eighteenth-Century Context' in P.J. Corish (ed.) *Radicals, Rebels and Establishment* (Belfast, 1985), pp 91-113.

——, 'Catholics under the Penal Laws' in *Eighteenth Century Ireland*, i (1986), pp 23-36.

——, 'The 1798 Rebellion in Wexford: United Irish Organisation, Membership, Leadership' in Whelan (ed.), *Wexford*, pp 248-95.

——, 'The Political Structures of the Defenders' in Gough and Dickson (eds.), *Ireland and the French Revolution*, pp 117-38.

——, 'Catholic Social Classes under the Penal Laws' in Power and Whelan (eds.), *Endurance and Emergence*, pp 57-84.

——, 'Burke, Ireland and Revolution; in *Eighteenth-Century Life*, xvi (1992), pp 21-42.

——, 'The Internal Politics of the United Irishmen' in Dickson, Keogh and Whelan (eds.), *United Irishmen*, pp 176-96.

——, 'Politics and Rebellion in Wicklow in the 1790s' in Ken Hannigan and William Nolan (eds.), *Wicklow: History and Society* (Dublin 1994), pp 411-501.

Curtin, Nancy, 'The transformation of the Society of United Irishmen into a Mass-Based Revolutionary Organisation 1794-6, in *I.H.S.*, xxiv (1985), pp 463-72.

——, *The United Irishmen: Popular Politics in Ulster and Dublin 1791-1798* (Oxford 1994).

——, 'Centres of Motion: Irish Cities and the Origins of Popular Politics' in Bergeron and Cullen (eds.), *Culture et pratiques*, pp 101-22.

Dickson, David, Introduction to Richard Musgrave, *Memoirs of Various Rebellions in Ireland* (repr. Fort Wayne, 1995).

——, Keogh, Dáire and Whelan, Kevin (eds.) *The United Irishmen: Radicalism, Republicanism and Rebellion* (Dublin, 1993).

Elliott, Marianne, *Partners in Revolution: The United Irishmen and France* (New Haven, 1982).

——, 'The Defenders in Ulster' in Dickson, Keogh and Whelan (eds.) *United Irishmen*, pp 222-33.

Farrell, William, *Carlow in '98: The Autobiography of William Farrell* (ed.) Roger McHugh (Dublin, 1949).

Froude, James Anthony, *The English in Ireland in the Eighteenth Century*, 3 vols. (London, 1872-74).

Furlong, Nicholas, *Father John Murphy of Boolavogue 1753-1798* (Dublin, 1992).

Gahan, Daniel, 'The Military Strategy of the Wexford United Irishmen in 1798' in *History Ireland*, no. 4 (1993), pp 28-32.

——, *The People's Rising, Wexford 1798* (Dublin, 1995).

Gordon, James, *History of the Rebellion in Ireland in year 1798,* (Dublin, 1801).

Gough, Hugh and Dickson, David (eds.), *Ireland and the French Revolution*, (Dublin, 1990).

Graham, Thomas, 'An Union of Power: The United Irish Organisation in Dickson, Keogh and Whelan (eds.), *United Irishmen*, pp 244-55.

Hay, Edward, *History of the Insurrection in the County of Wexford, A.D. 1798* (Dublin, 1803).

Holt, Joseph, *Memoirs*, ed. T.C. Croker, 2 vols. (London, 1838).

Kavanagh, Patrick, *A Popular History of the Insurrection of 1798* (Dublin, 1870).

Keogh, Dáire, *The French Disease: The Catholic Church and Radicalism in Ireland 1790-1800* (Dublin, 1993).

——, 'The battle for affection; Catholics, radicals and reaction, 1790-1800', in *Bullán* (1995).

Lecky, W.E.H., *History of Ireland in the Eighteenth Century*, 5 vols. (London, 1892).

Madden, R.R., *The United Irishmen, their Lives and Times*, 7 vols. (London, 1842-6).

O'Dea, Michael and Whelan, Kevin (eds.), *Nations and Nationalisms: France, Britain, Ireland and the Eighteenth Century Context* (Oxford, 1995).

Power, T.P., *Land, Politics and Society in Eighteenth-Century Tipperary* (Oxford, 1993).

—— and Whelan, Kevin (eds.), *Endurance and Emergence: Catholics in Ireland in the Eighteenth Century* (Dublin, 1990).

Ronan, M.V. (ed.), *Personal Recollections of Wexford and Wicklow Insurgents of 1798 as collected by the Rev. Luke Cullen 1798-1859* (Enniscorthy, 1958).

Russell, Thomas, *Journals and Memoirs*, (ed.) C.J. Woods (Dublin, 1991).

Smyth, Jim, *The Men of No Property: Irish Radicals and Popular Politics in the late Eighteenth Century* (Dublin, 1992).

Stewart, A.T.Q., *A Deeper Silence: The Hidden Origins of the United Irishmen* (London, 1993).

——, *The Summer Soldiers. The 1798 Rebellion in Antrim and Down* (Belfast, 1995).

[Tone, Theobald Wolfe], *An Argument on behalf of the Catholics of Ireland* (Dublin, 1791).

Veritas, *The State of His Majesty's Subjects in Ireland professing the Roman Catholic Religion* (2nd ed., Dublin, 1799).

A Vindication of the Roman Catholic Clergy of the Town of Wexford during the Unhappy Rebellion (Dublin, 1799).

Walsh, Walter, 'Religion, Ethnicity and History: Clues to the Cultural Construction of Law' in Ronald Bayor and T.J. Meagher (eds), *The New York Irish* (Baltimore, 1995) pp 48-69.

Whelan, Kevin, 'The Role of the Catholic Priest in the 1798 Rebellion in County Wexford' in Whelan (ed.), *Wexford*, pp 296-315.

——, 'Politicisation in County Wexford and the origins of the 1798 Rebellion' in Gough and Dickson (eds.), *Ireland and the French Revolution*, pp 156-78.

——, 'The Catholic Community in Eighteenth-Century County Wexford' in Power and Whelan (eds.), *Endurance and Emergence*, pp 156-78.

——, 'Catholic Mobilisation 1750-1850' in Bergeron and Cullen (ed.) *Culture et practiques*, pp 235-58.

——, 'Catholics, Politicisation and the 1798 Rebellion' in Réamóinn Ó Muiri (ed.), *Irish Church History Today* (Armagh, 1991), pp 63-83.

——, *The Tree of Liberty: Radicalism, Catholicism and the Construction of Irish Identity, 1760-1830* (Cork, 1996).

Index